THE TOTAL JAZZ DRUMMER

>> A Fun and Comprehensive Overview of Jazz Drumming

SUNNY JAIN

Alfred, the leader in educational publishing,

and the National Guitar Workshop,

one of America's finest guitar schools, have joined

forces to bring you the best, most progressive

educational tools possible. We hope you will enjoy

this book and encourage you to look for

other fine products from Alfred and the

National Guitar Workshop.

Alfred Publishing Co., Inc.
16320 Roscoe Blvd., Suite 100
P.O. Box 10003
Van Nuys, CA 91410-0003
alfred.com

Copyright © MMVII by Alfred Publishing Co., Inc.
All rights reserved. Printed in USA.

ISBN-10: 0-7390-3852-4 (Book & CD)
ISBN-13: 978-0-7390-3852-9 (Book & CD)

This book was acquired, edited and produced
by Workshop Arts, Inc., the publishing arm of
the National Guitar Workshop.
Nathaniel Gunod, acquisitions, managing editor
Burgess Speed, editor, interior photography
Matthew Liston, assistant editor
Timothy Phelps, interior design
Ante Gelo, music typesetter
CD recorded by Collin Tilton at Bar None Studio, Northford, CT

Cover photograph: © istockphoto.com/Kuzma
Drum photograph courtesy Slingerland/Gibson USA

Table of Contents

About the Author 4
   Acknowledgements 4
Introduction 5

Part 1: The Beginning Jazz Drummer 6
   Practicing 6

Chapter 1: The Basics 7
   Match Grip vs. Traditional Grip 7
   Fulcrum and Motion 8
   Understanding Rhythm 9
   The 26 Standard American
       Drum Rudiments 12

Chapter 2: Getting Into the Drumset 21
   The Setup 21
   Sitting at the Drumset 22
   Tuning 22

Chapter 3: The Basic Jazz Rhythm 23
   The Swing Feel 23
   The Swing Pattern 23
   Basic Independence 26
   Syncopation 28

Chapter 4: The Various Styles of Jazz 29
   Second Line or Street Beat 29
   The Jazz Waltz 30
   Latin Rhythms 31
   Afro-Cuban Rhythms 33
   Straight Eighth Cymbal Patterns 44

Part 2: The Intermediate Jazz Drummer 45
   Practicing 45

Chapter 5: The Art of Brushes 46
   Brush Strokes 46
   Brush Patterns 48

Chapter 6: Playing Tempos 54
   Different Tempos 54

Chapter 7: Coordination 55
   Four-Way Coordination 55

Chapter 8: Fills and Soloing 70
   In the Style of Max Roach 73
   In the Style of "Philly" Joe Jones 75
   In the Style of Elvin Jones 77
   In the Style of Tony Williams 81

Part 3: The Advanced Jazz Drummer 83
    Practicing 83

Chapter 9: Linear Phrasing 84
    Snare Drum Accents 86
    Bass Drum and Cymbal Accents 94
    Linear Phrasing with the Ride Cymbal......... 102

Chapter 10: Odd Time Meters........................ 110
    Odd Time Exercises 110
    $\frac{5}{4}$ Swing 111
    $\frac{5}{4}$ Latin 112
    $\frac{7}{4}$ Swing 113
    $\frac{7}{4}$ Latin 114

Chapter 11: Rhythmic Grouping........................ 115

Chapter 12: Polyrhythms 116
    Polyrhythmic Ratios 116
    The Rhythm Table 119

Chapter 13: Polyrhythmic Limbs........................ 120

Appendix 122
    Improvisation................................... 122
    Professional Advice 123
    Outro 123

Listening Guide.. 124

Sunny Jain Discography.. 127

About the Author

Photo by Bernardo Borghetti

Sunny Jain was born and raised in Rochester, New York and began percussion studies at the age of 10. Shortly after receiving his first drumset at age 13, he fell in love with jazz. Sunny has since gone on to earn a Bachelor of Music degree in jazz studies from Rutgers University and a Master of Arts in music business from New York University. In the past 10 years, Sunny has been on faculty at Staten Island Academy and National Guitar Workshop, and has guest lectured at a variety of educational institutions. In 2002, he was selected as a *Jazz Ambassador* by the U.S. Department of State and the Kennedy Center. From 2002–2003, he worked in the education department of *Jazz at Lincoln Center*. For the past six years, Sunny has been the drummer for Hayes Greenfield's Jazz-A-Ma-Tazz, an interactive music show for children.

Making New York City his home for the past eight years, Sunny Jain is a leading voice for the new music of *Indo-Jazz* (jazz music fused with music from India). Since its inception in 2002, the Sunny Jain Collective has received international critical acclaim. The group has performed throughout the U.S. and has toured India three times, headlining at all the major festivals there. In June 2005, *Jazz Hot* magazine (France) featured Sunny and noted him as a rising star for his fusion of jazz and Indian music. Sunny Jain Collective has released 3 CD's thus far: *Avaaz* (Sinj Records 2006); *Mango Festival* (ZoHo Music 2004); *As Is* (NCM East 2002).

Sunny has performed with several world-renowned artists such as Kiran Ahluwalia, Eric Alexander, Joey Baron, Kenny Barron, Seamus Blake, Ted Dunbar, Kyle Eastwood, Gerald Cleaver, Norah Jones, Lonnie Plaxico and Kenny Wollesen. He has toured Europe, Japan, India, West Africa, Canada and the United States. Sunny was a recipient of the Arts International grant in both 2003 and 2004, which supported international touring efforts. He also received Chamber Music America's New Works Grant in 2006, which is awarded to adventurous composers.

To find out more about Sunny Jain, please visit: www.jainsounds.com.

Acknowledgements

Thank you to all those that made this project possible: to Burgess Speed, Nat Gunod, David Smolover, Paula Abate, David Moreno and everyone else at National Guitar Workshop and DayJams; to Alfred Publishing; to Collin Tilton at Bar None Studios; to Noah Baerman for his guidance during my writing process; to Hayes Greenfield for being so passionate about education and the youth; to my teachers, Rich Thompson, Bobby Thomas, Kenny Barron, the late Ted Dunbar, Ralph Bowen, Akira Tana, Michael Carvin and Paramjyoti Kocherlakota for sharing so much knowledge, but for mainly reinforcing my love for music; to my family and especially to my one and only, Sapana, for her tremendous amount of support and love.

Introduction

Welcome to *The Total Jazz Drummer*. This book is a comprehensive guide to jazz drumming for the beginning to advanced student. After establishing the fundamentals of drumming, this book will introduce you to the essence of jazz: swing. Through a series of coordination exercises, brush techniques and solo ideas, you will gain a solid foundation in jazz drumming. One book cannot possibly teach *everything* you need to know about jazz; this book aims to cover the crucial elements needed for you to play this music. Although you can learn much from this book alone, it is highly suggested that you also study with a teacher in order to help you with the nuances of jazz drumming. Moreover, if you really want to be able to play jazz, you must listen to the music. It is essential that you experience this music live as well as listen to recordings.

Some suggestions for using this book:

- Be creative once you've learned any given exercise. Come up with your own ways of interpreting or expanding an exercise into something else. Improvisation is essential to jazz, and it is crucial to the learning process that you approach this material in a creative manner. Don't just play an exercise and move on. Think: "What else can I do with this rhythm?"

- Go back and practice exercises even after you've moved on to another chapter. Again, you might discover new ways of approaching them, but more importantly, it's a good idea to occasionally practice old material so that it is not forgotten.

- Practice the exercises using various dynamics, from soft to loud, and various tempos, from slow to fast. Suggested tempo markings will be indicated at the beginning of exercises.

- Use the accompanying CD so that you can hear how certain exercises are supposed to sound.

- Have fun.

Note: This book is written from a right-handed perspective. If you are left-handed, you may reverse instructions involving the left and right hand, as well as the placement (left to right or right to left) of the parts of your drumset.

Track 0.0 — A compact disc is available with this book. Using the disc will help make learning more enjoyable and the information more meaningful. Listening to the CD will help you correctly interpret the rhythms and feel of each example. The symbol to the left appears next to each example that is performed on the CD. Example numbers are above the symbol. The track number below each symbol corresponds directly to the song or example you want to hear. In most cases, there is more than one example per track; this is reflected in the track numbers (for example: track 2.1, track 2.2, track 2.3, etc.). Enjoy.

PART 1: The Beginning Jazz Drummer

Let's start by defining some basic musical terms.

Beat—the basic rhythmic unit in a piece of music.

Rhythm—a pattern formed by a series of short and long sounds and silences.

Tempo or *Time*—the measurement of the speed of rhythm.

Metronome—a device used to count time with precision. Various tempos can be set and are indicated through aural or visual signals.

Measure or *Bar*—a subdivision of rhythm into groups of multiple beats.

Practicing

As a drummer, your primary function is to provide a solid rhythmic foundation. To achieve this, it is important to develop and use good practice techniques. Here are some suggestions on how to practice the exercises in this book:

- Practice using a metronome.

- Count aloud while playing. This is essential for becoming a good reader.

- Break up measures and go over sections individually. Then, put them all back together.

- Practice for a specific amount of time on a regular basis as opposed to long practice sessions infrequently. For example, practice 30 minutes a day, five days a week, not once a week for two hours.

- Practice at various tempos from slow to fast. If you practice with a metronome, you will see that playing at slow tempos is just as hard as playing at fast tempos.

- Practice with relaxed muscles and avoid tensing up. Your body and muscles must feel loose in order for your sticks to respond effectively to the drums.

- Breathe just as you normally do. Don't develop bad habits of irregular breathing patterns or holding your breath while playing certain rhythms.

Remember, "practice makes perfect" or in reality, "almost perfect."

Chapter 1: The Basics

To get the most out of this book, you should have a basic understanding of drums, rhythm and reading music. Part I will help you brush up on all the fundamentals you need to get started.

Match Grip vs. Traditional Grip

Match grip.

Traditional grip.

There are many theories about the best way to hold the sticks, especially when it comes to jazz. Following is a brief history of the grips and their applications.

Drums (in various forms) have been used in many cultures as far back as 6000 B.C. Their main purposes were for ceremonial use and for communication. Until the early eighteenth century, drums were either played by hand or with sticks. When using sticks, the grip used was the *match grip*, and sensibly so. If without any thought you picked up some sticks, how would you pick them up? With match grip, both your hands hold the sticks in the same manner, as demonstrated in the picture above.

It wasn't until the early eighteenth century and the advent of the marching field drum (which hangs at one's side) that a new grip was developed: *traditional grip*. With traditional grip (depending upon if you're right- or left-handed), your "strong" hand is the same as in match grip, but your "weak" hand holds the stick as shown in the picture. The back end of the stick is held between the thumb and index finger and then rests between your middle fingers.

The traditional grip, as we now know it, was devised as a logical answer to playing a drum slung at the side, but was never intended for jazz drumming. After all, the birth of the drumset occurred in the late nineteenth century, and that's also around the time when jazz started to form.

Many teachers still teach that traditional grip is the correct grip to play jazz. However, unless you are marching with a field drum by your side, it makes perfect sense to grip the sticks the same way with each hand (match grip).

If you want to become a well-rounded drummer/percussionist (outside just being a jazz drummer), you should learn both grips. The grip you choose to use is your preference, and contrary to popular belief, will not hinder your speed or volume on the drums.

Fulcrum and Motion

The *fulcrum* is the point where the stick is balanced without the aid of other fingers and can achieve maximum rebound from the drum.

To learn more about fulcrum and motion, you may be interested in researching the *Moeller Technique*. The Moeller Technique (which is beyond the scope of this book) was designed to improve the physics of your grip, enabling you to play with speed and comfort.

Match Grip

The fulcrum for match grip is between the pads of the index finger and the thumb. The wrist motion for match grip should be up and down with your palm facing down, similar to turning off a light switch. However, when you switch to playing the ride cymbal, your thumb should be on top of the stick.

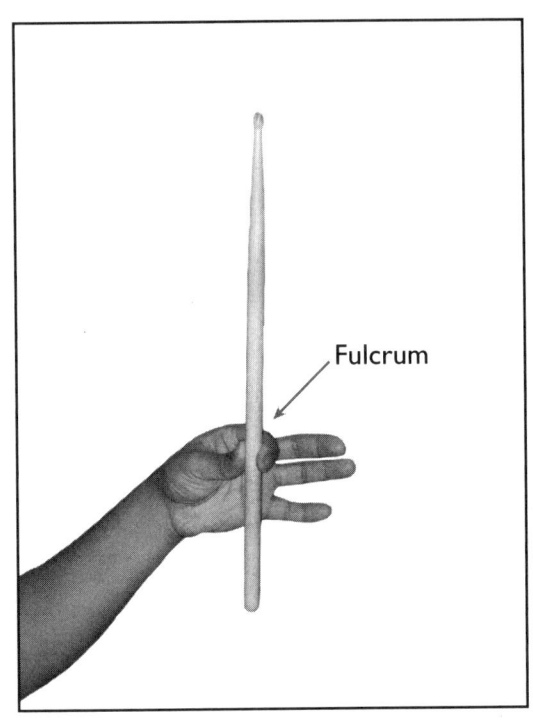

Fulcrum for match grip.

Traditional Grip

Again, depending upon if you're right-handed or left-handed, your "strong" hand is the same as in match grip, but your "weak" hand holds the stick as shown in the picture. The fulcrum is in the webbing or pocket between the thumb and your index finger. The wrist motion with this hand should be similar to turning a doorknob.

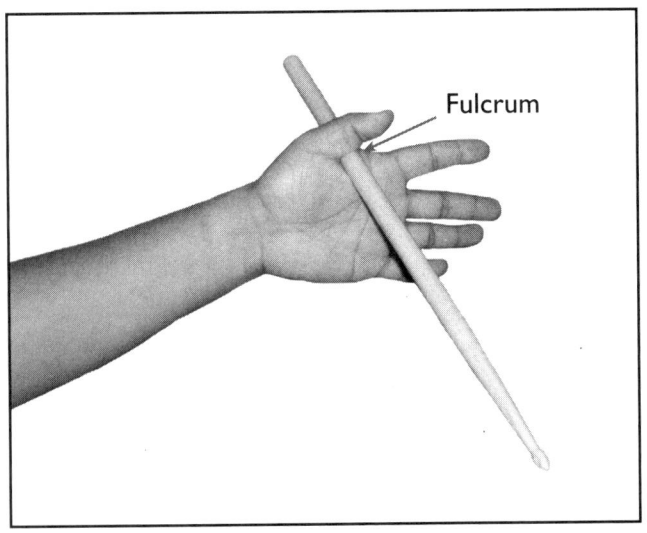

Fulcrum for traditional grip.

Understanding Rhythm

Note and Rest Values

Understanding rhythm is essentially a mathematical exercise, mainly dealing with fractions and ratios. Rhythm is notated with *notes* (musical notation for making sound) and *rests* (musical notation for silence) of precise durations or *values*.

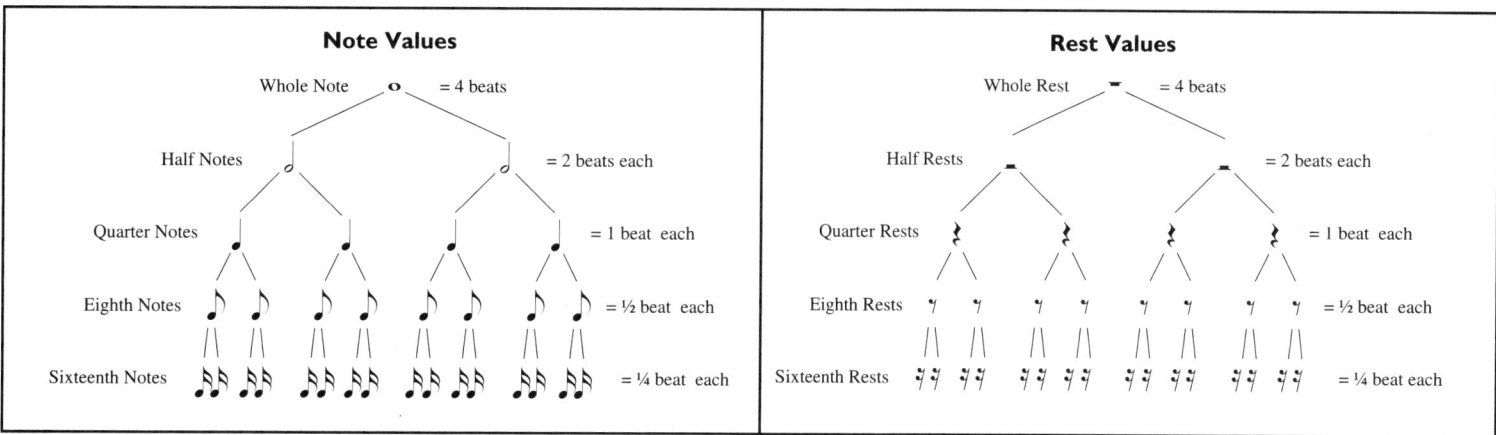

Time Signatures

The note and rest values in the charts above are true for most of the rhythms in this book. However, these can change depending on the *time signature* or *meter*. A time signature consists of two numerals placed at the beginning of a piece of music. The bottom number tells us the kind of note that equals one beat. The top number tells us how many of those beats total one measure.

A time signature groups musical notations on a *staff*, which is a set of five horizontal lines on which musical notation is placed to indicate *pitch* (the highness or lowness of a sound) and rhythm. The *neutral clef* ‖ is used to notate drum music, where each line of the staff represents a different drum or cymbal instead of a pitch.

A *bar line* is a vertical line which separates the music into measures or bars. A *double bar line* denotes the beginning or end of a musical idea or *phrase*. *Repeat signs* indicate the music between them should be played twice. If there is only one repeat sign, go back to the beginning of the music and play it a second time from the start.

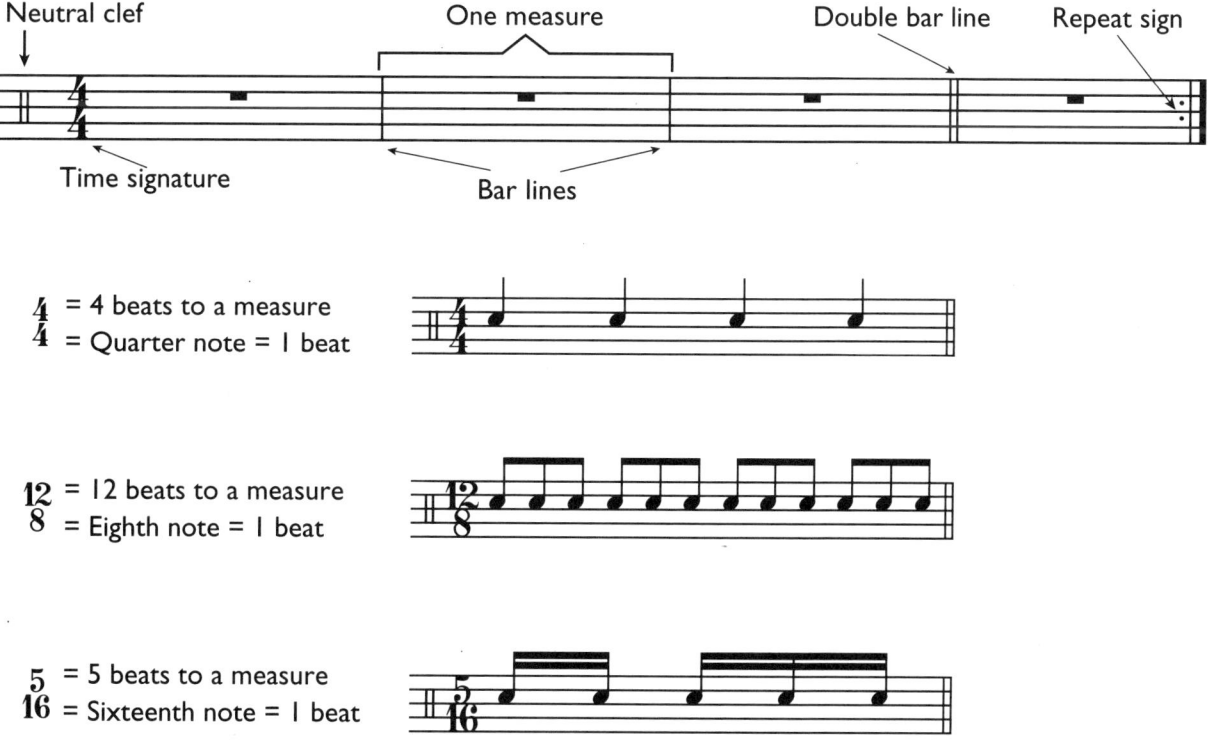

The Total Jazz Drummer   9

Dots

A *dot* after a note or rest increases its value by one half.

For example, a *dotted half note* equals 3 beats.

A *dotted quarter note* equals 1 ½ beats.

A *dotted eighth rest* equals ¾ of beat of silence.

Triplets

At this point, it is essential as a beginning jazz drummer to understand *triplets*. The triplet is the basis for the jazz rhythm and feel. A triplet is one beat divided equally into three notes or rests. For example, the value of one half note equals that of three quarter-note triplets. The value of one quarter note equals that of three eighth-note triplets. See the following chart for triplet breakdown relations.

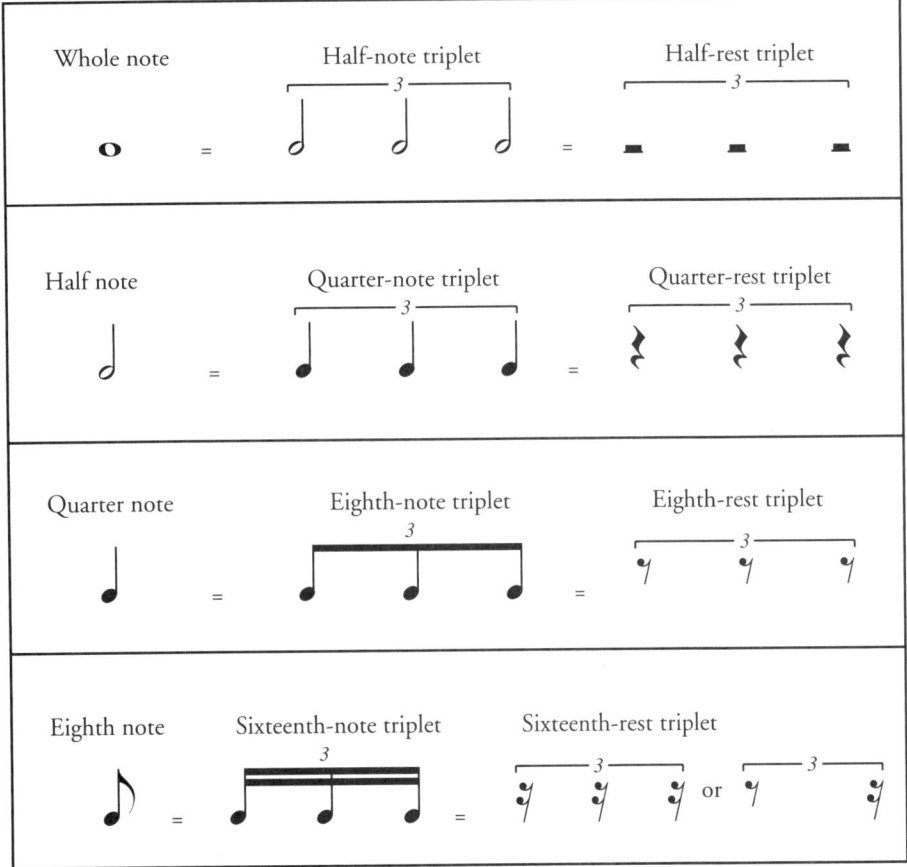

Counting and Subdividing

Now, let's put all these parts together and count out some rhythms. Remember, rhythm is the same sound or beat repeated over and over in a uniform pattern—similar to the steadiness of walking or jogging, or the beating of our heart. So, counting should be done in this same consistent manner.

Subdividing (breaking down into smaller components) and counting a rhythm can help tremendously in your ability to play that rhythm on the drums; it is highly suggested. Following are some basic rules for counting and subdividing. In $\frac{4}{4}$ time, quarter notes are counted with beat numbers (1, 2, 3, 4, etc.); eighth notes are counted with "&" indicating the upbeat (1-&, 2-&, 3-&, 4-&, etc.); triplets are counted by dividing each beat into three equal parts (1 trip-let, 2 trip-let, etc.); and sixteenth notes are counted by dividing each beat into four equal parts (1-e-&-ah, 2-e-&-ah, etc.).

The following rhythms should be counted against a metronome click.

In $\frac{12}{8}$ time, the eighth note receives one beat, so the counting has to be adjusted as follows.

In $\frac{5}{16}$ time, the sixteenth note receives one beat, so the counting must be adjusted in the following way.

The Total Jazz Drummer   11

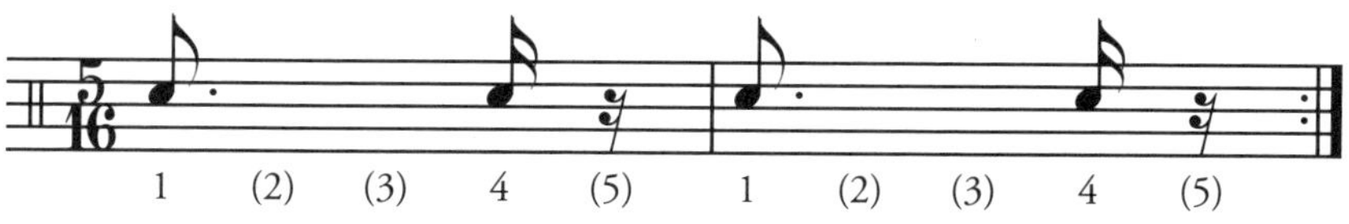

The 26 Standard American Drum Rudiments

Drum rudiments are the first elements needed for playing the drums. For instance, when learning a language, one must learn the alphabet and then the words that are formed from it. The more advanced a person's vocabulary becomes in a given language, the better equipped one is to communicate in that language. Learning the 26 standard American drum rudiments is the first step in learning the language of drumming.

The following rudiments should be practiced by starting or leading with your right hand and then with your left hand. Practice at various metronome markings.

R = Right hand
L = Left hand

1) Single-Stroke Roll

In the first rudiment, alternate stickings from slow to fast, striving for a consistent sound from one hand to the other.

2) Long Roll/Double-Stroke Roll

Strike the drum with the first stroke and achieve the second stroke through a rebound or bounce as you're coming off the drum. Alternate this between hands from slow to fast. Strive for a consistent sound from one hand to the next and from stroke to bounce.

Note that the last bar indicates a double stroke roll as fast as you can play it.

12 The Total Jazz Drummer

The following rolls consist of the double-stroke roll ending or beginning with an *accent* (a note played louder than the others).

> = *Accent*

3) 5-Stroke Roll

R R L L R   L L R R L   etc.

R LL RR L   RR LL etc.

Indicates two hits with one stroke. The first hit is through the stroke, and the second is through the natural bounce.

4) 7-Stroke Roll

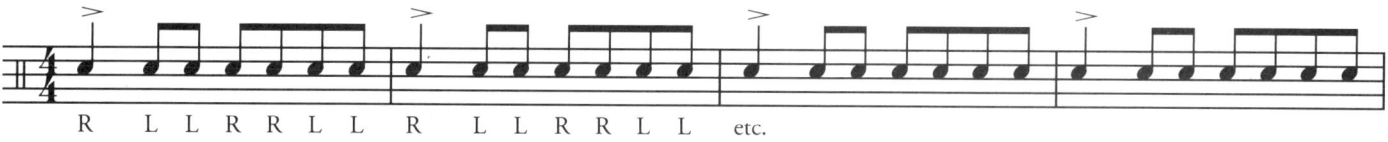

R L L R R L L   R L L R R L L   etc.

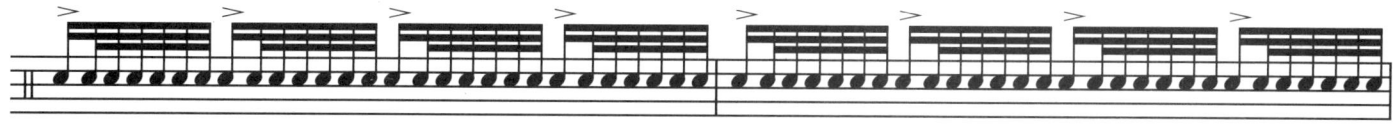

R LL RR LL L RR LL RR etc.   R LL RR LL R LL RR LL etc.

The Total Jazz Drummer

5) 9-Stroke Roll

6) 10-Stroke Roll

7) 11-Stroke Roll

8) 13-Stroke Roll

etc.

9) 15-Stroke Roll

10) Single Paradiddle

The *single paradiddle* is played just like it sounds:
"par-a-did-dle."

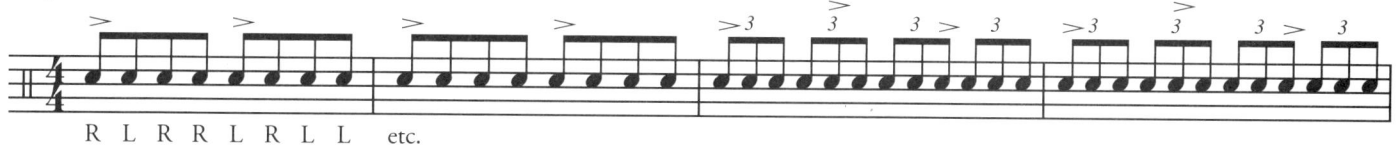

11) Double Paradiddle

The *double paradiddle* is played just like it sounds:
"dou-ble par-a-did-dle."

The Total Jazz Drummer   15

12) Flam

The *flam* is similar to the single stroke roll, except that a *grace note* precedes each stroke. A grace note is played much softer than the strokes and is achieved by simply letting the opposite stick drop a split second before the main stroke is played. The sticking is indicated with lower and upper case letters (lR, rL, etc.).

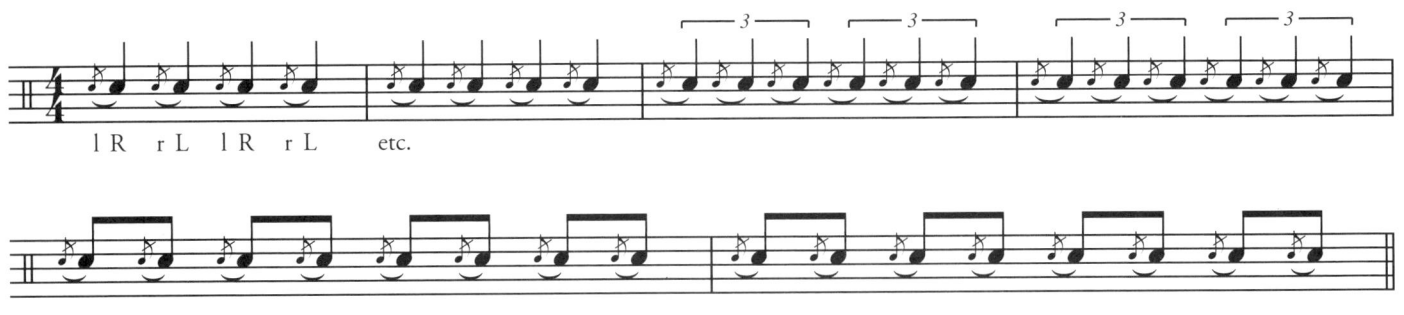

lR   rL   lR   rL   etc.

13) Flam Accent

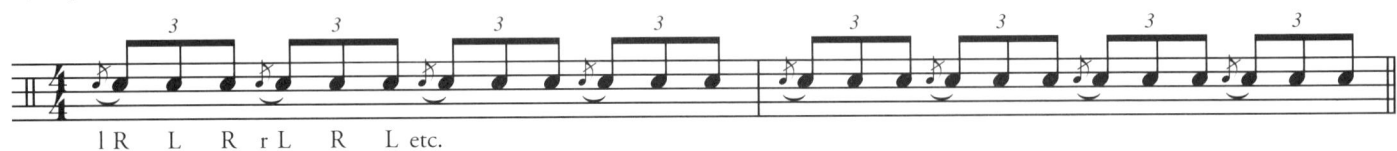

lR   L   R   rL   R   L etc.

14) Flam Tap

lR   R   rL   L   etc.

15) Flam Paradiddle or Flamadiddle

lR   L   R   R   rL   R   L   L   etc.

16 The Total Jazz Drummer

16) Flam Paradiddle-diddle

17) Ruff or Half-Drag

The *ruff* should be played as a grace note or *pick-up* to the stroke and employs the double stroke.

18) Single Drag

19) Double Drag

20) Drag Paradiddle No. 1

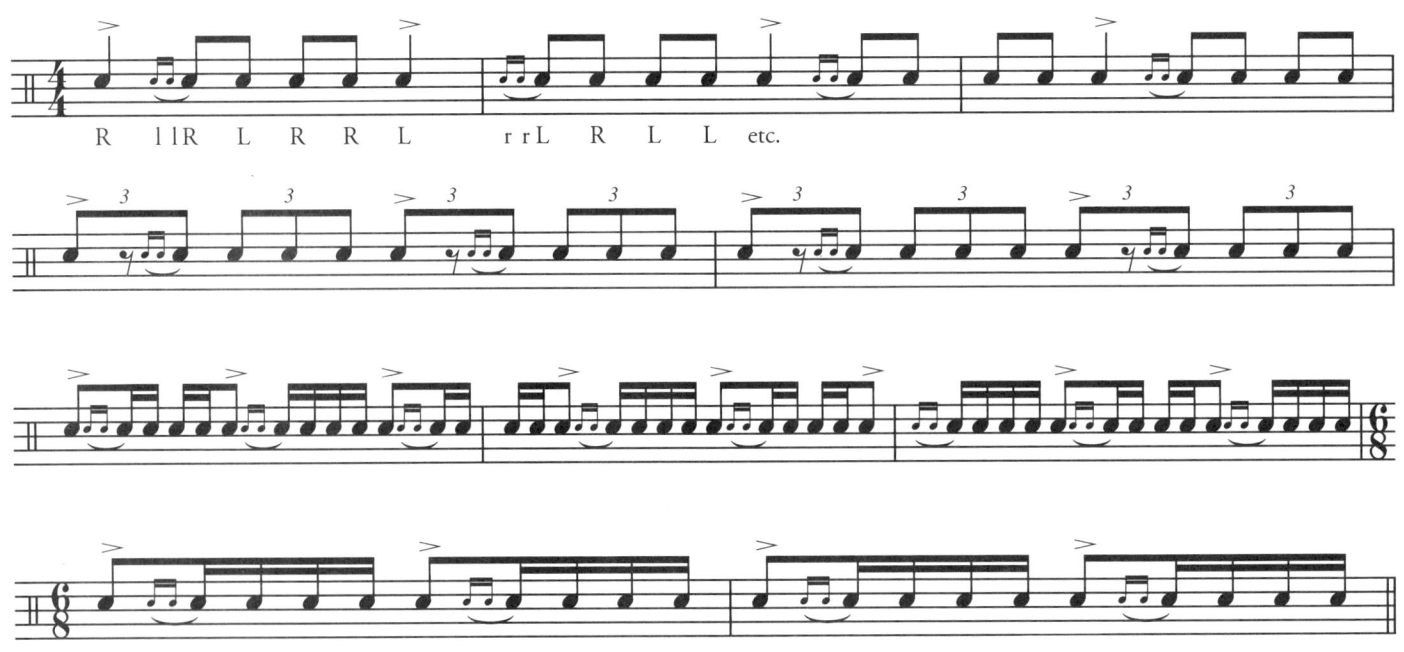

21) Drag Paradiddle No. 2

26) Flamacue

L R L R L R etc.

> **Note:** There are other rudiments worth looking into on your own, such as Swiss rudiments and various double-stroke rolls. These are good to know but are not considered to be part of the 26 standard American drum rudiments.

20   The Total Jazz Drummer

Chapter 2: Getting Into the Drumset

Interestingly enough, you are about to study the music that was the main impetus for the creation of the *drumset*—jazz. The drumset, or *trap set*, came into being at the end of the nineteenth century with the creation of the bass drum pedal. This allowed one person to sit down and play multiple drums simultaneously. It then became increasingly popular alongside the formation and growth of jazz music in the early twentieth century.

Below is the legend for drumset notation. This key is based on a traditional four-piece jazz drumset.

Drumset Notational Key

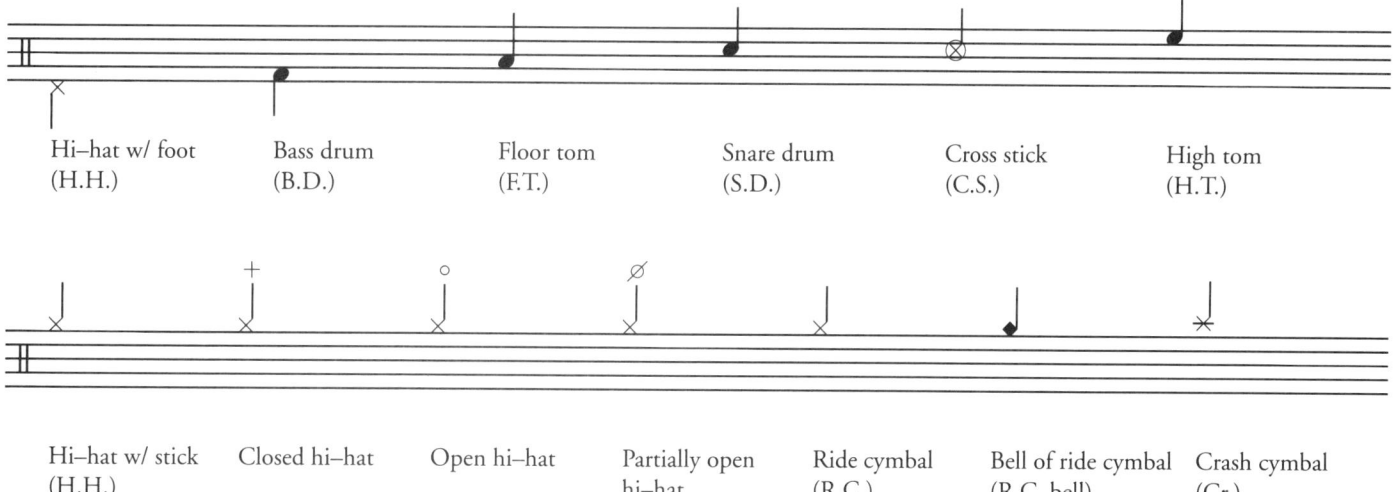

Hi–hat w/ foot (H.H.) | Bass drum (B.D.) | Floor tom (F.T.) | Snare drum (S.D.) | Cross stick (C.S.) | High tom (H.T.)

Hi–hat w/ stick (H.H.) | Closed hi–hat | Open hi–hat | Partially open hi–hat | Ride cymbal (R.C.) | Bell of ride cymbal (R.C. bell) | Crash cymbal (Cr.)

The Setup

Now, before we start playing the drums, let's cover the basics of setting them up and sitting at them.

The pictures below show the setup we will be working with in the following pages. The basic four-piece drumset includes a snare drum (1), bass drum (2), high tom (3), floor tom (4), hi-hat (5), ride cymbal (6) and crash cymbal (7).

Drumset from the front.

Drumset from the back.

The Total Jazz Drummer

Sitting at the Drumset

- Your physical stature and the length of your legs have a lot to do with the appropriate height of your drum *throne,* or drum seat. So, experiment with setting the throne at different heights and see which one allows you to play with the most ease. A general rule of thumb, however, is to sit at your drum throne so that your thighs are parallel to the ground.

- Sit on the front edge of the drum throne. This forces you to sit up straight, have good posture and to not lean backward or forward.

- Set up the drums so that everything is in fair reach and you're not stretching too far to reach any drum or cymbal. Imagine that you're at a telephone switchboard and you have to keep plugging and unplugging connections. You want to accomplish this effortlessly. Forget about the pictures and videos you've seen of drummers reaching six feet in the air to hit a cymbal. That's about theatrics and not drumming.

- If you're playing traditional grip, remember to tilt your snare drum about 30 degrees to the right (as seen in the picture on page 21). If you're playing match grip, the snare drum should be flat.

- Sit in front of the drumset in a relaxed manner, as if you were sitting at the table eating dinner. Your shoulders should be down and arms by your sides.

- Maintain your instrument. Make sure all heads are tuned evenly and not too loose or too tight. Strive to get a good sound out of your instrument and treat it with care.

Tuning

Tuning the drums is a matter of personal taste, but nonetheless requires careful consideration. The first step in tuning your drums is to make sure that all your lug nuts are tightened to the same degree (this is done with the aid of your drum *key)*. If they are not, you risk warping your drum head, getting an unbalanced sound from the drum and sacrificing the natural bounce you should be able to achieve from striking the drum. Also, both heads (the bottom and top) on a drum should be tuned to the same pitch; otherwise you will not get an even tone, but overtones that will disturb the quality of the sound. Then again, this might be your preference.

By the nature of your drums, the bass drum should be the lowest sounding drum, next is your floor tom and then your rack tom. Your snare should be the highest pitched drum with the snare turned off. (There is a lever on the side of the snare that disengages the *snares* from the bottom drum head.) Experiment with pitches and listen to other jazz drummers. Some prefer to tune the toms very high while keeping the bass drum loose so as get a tone from that as well. Others prefer to tune toms very low and stuff the bass drum with a pillow so it doesn't ring. There is a plethora of sounds and tunings you can get from your drums, but make sure you approach them with care.

Chapter 3: The Basic Jazz Rhythm

Jazz has its roots in New Orleans in the late nineteenth century. You should acquaint yourself with the music's history to gain insight into the exercises you are about to learn and to further your understanding of jazz. Moreover, you should be listening to jazz music to internalize its feel and develop an appreciation for it. The only way to develop the feel of a jazz drummer is to listen to the drum masters, like "Papa" Jo Jones, "Philly" Joe Jones, Max Roach, Elvin Jones, Tony Williams, etc. These drummers, and others, were pivotal in shaping this music and establishing the drum language.

For suggested listening, refer to the Listening Guide section at the end of this book (page 124).

The Swing Feel

Swing, the cornerstone of jazz rhythm and feel, is based on the *triplet feel*. Whereas *straight* eighth notes or sixteenth notes (something that you hear in rock music) constitute a *duple* (groups of 2) feel, "swung" eighth notes are generated by the triplet (groups of 3) feel. This type of triplet or swing feel is also known as *shuffle rhythm*.

Note: An extra beat is added at the end of each recorded example for a sense of finality.

The Swing Pattern

The *swing pattern* is the single most important element of the jazz rhythm and the first area of importance in developing your jazz feel. The swing pattern accents all of the quarter-note *downbeats*, with the *upbeats* or *skip beats* (beats in between the downbeats) acting as the pick-ups to the quarter-note downbeats.

Here's the basic swing jazz ride cymbal pattern:

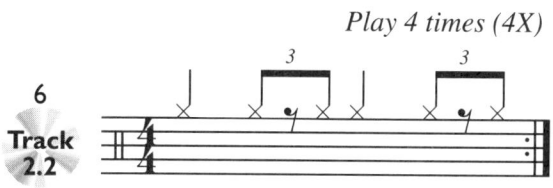

You may also see the jazz ride cymbal pattern notated like this:

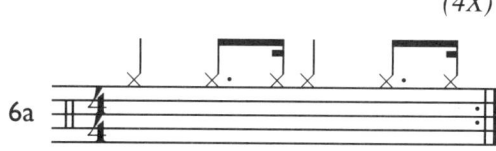

You can also play the jazz pattern on the hi-hat:

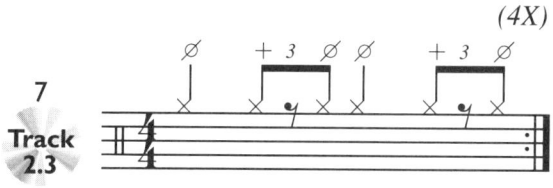

Or:

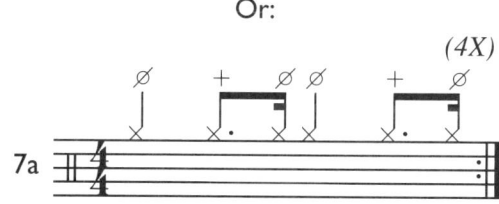

The Total Jazz Drummer   23

Now, don't be confused by the different notations of the jazz pattern. They are both supposed to sound the same and have that "swinging" or triplet feel. However, when you are playing the swing pattern at a very fast tempo, it feels and sounds like straight eighth notes, like this:

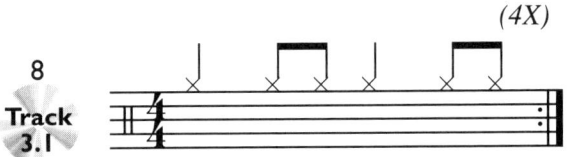

For the sake of really grasping the triplet feel, the jazz pattern will only be notated in triplet subdivisions in Section 1. However, in the later sections of this book, you will see the jazz pattern notated in the various ways mentioned.

Again, let's listen to the difference between straight eighth notes and swung eighth notes.

Some teachers and/or books suggest that you should accent the ride cymbal only on beats 2 and 4, but that is incorrect. As you'll soon see, beats 2 and 4 will be accented naturally, and thinking about the jazz ride pattern as a constant quarter note pulse gives the rhythm forward motion. Remember, the goal is for your ride pattern to have that triplet, buoyant feel. "Papa" Jo Jones, Max Roach and "Philly" Joe Jones had some of the cleanest, swinging ride cymbal patterns in jazz drumming history. As a beginning jazz drummer, you are strongly advised to listen to these drummers as an introduction to ride cymbal feels. Think about playing your ride cymbal as if your stick was dancing off the cymbal. A phrase that is useful to sing along when playing is: "lang, spang-a-lang, spang-a-lang."

The Bass Drum

The next element we'll add to the swing pattern is the bass drum. The bass drum should be played lightly and should almost be felt and not heard. In jazz, we call this *feathering* the bass drum. Again, you don't want to play the bass drum as loudly as you would in rock drumming; jazz does not rely on a heavy, driving beat the way rock music does. The bass drum should not overwhelm the bass player or the rest of the band.

The example below adds the bass drum to the jazz ride pattern.

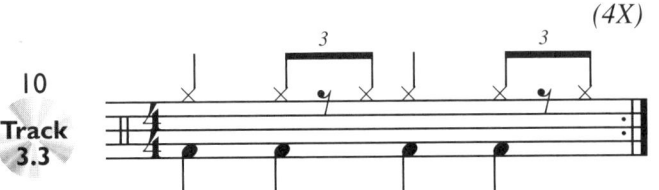

The Hi-Hat

Remember it was mentioned that beats 2 and 4 would naturally get accented? Well, that's the role of the hi-hat.

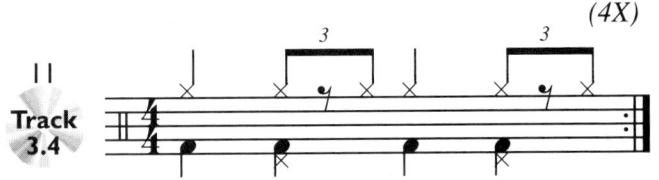

24   The Total Jazz Drummer

The Snare Drum

Now let's add the final limb, the left hand on the snare drum. For the basic jazz pattern, we'll have the left hand playing a *cross stick* on beat 4. A cross stick 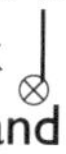 is accomplished by resting your stick across the drum and clicking the end of your stick against the rim of the drum (see photo below).

Cross sticking.

Listen to this example of cross sticking.

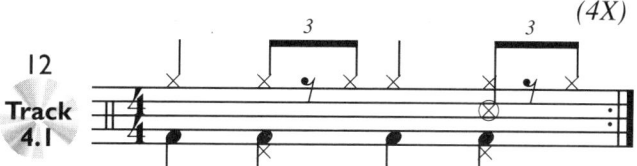

Now that you have the basic jazz pattern, let's look at variations you can play on the cymbal. The eventual goal is to feel loose and comfortable with your ride cymbal and be able to switch from pattern to pattern without thinking about it.

Cymbal Patterns

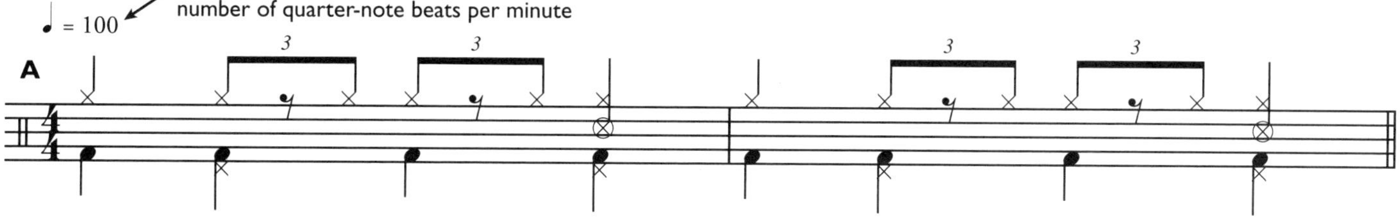

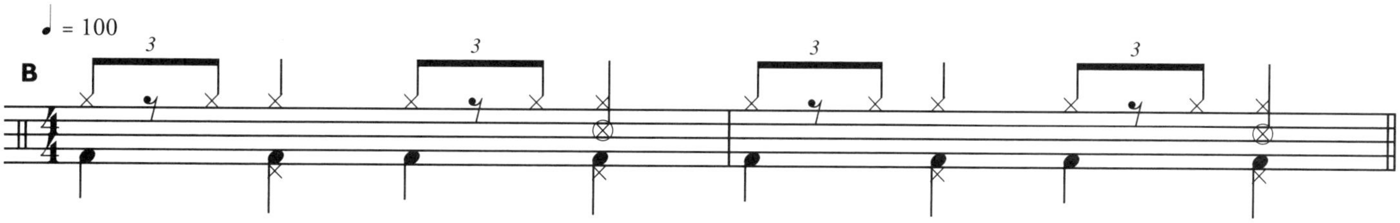

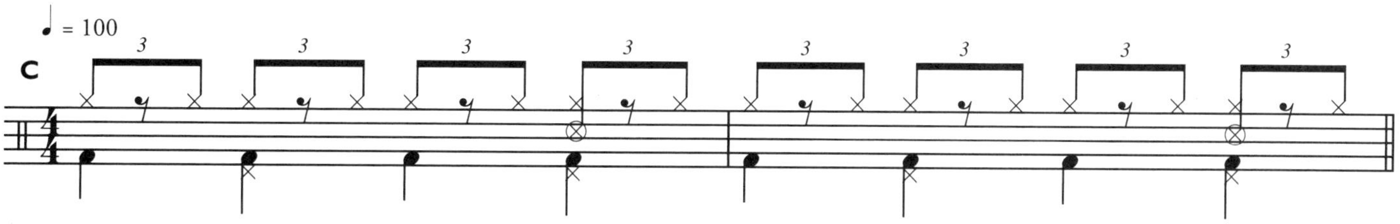

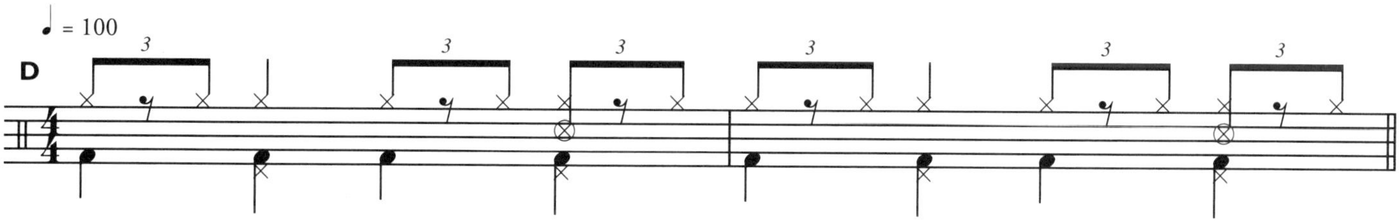

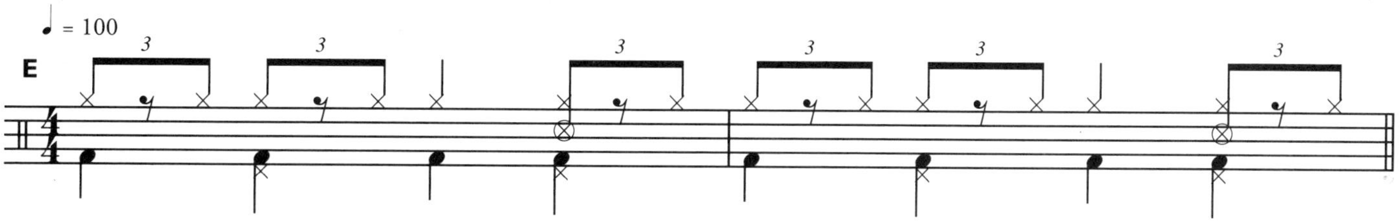

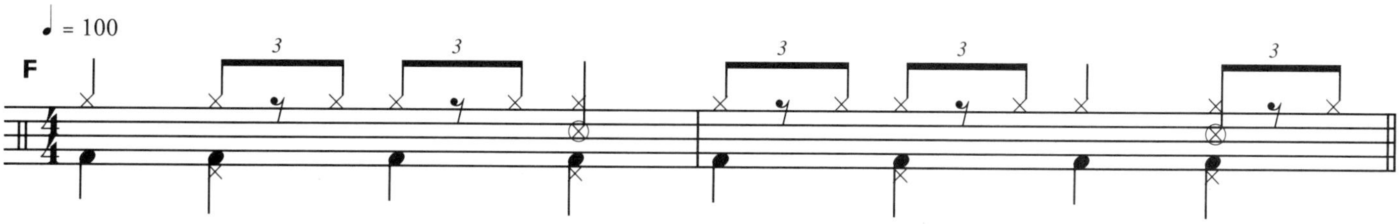

Basic Independence

The snare drum is capable of much more than just accenting beat 4 in the ride cymbal pattern. It is also used to *comp* (provide musical accompaniment) behind a soloist and add *embellishments*, or "flavor," to the basic jazz pattern. To begin our journey into *limb control* (playing different rhythms with each of your arms and legs) and independence, here are some snare drum exercises to practice while keeping the jazz pattern going. The ride cymbal is written out for each example with the snare drum for you to see where the hits line up. Remember to treat all eighth notes as swung.

The bass drum and hi-hat, although not written in the following exercises, will keep this constant rhythm throughout:

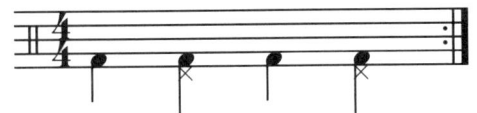

Basic Independence Exercises

26   The Total Jazz Drummer

Now, go back to the Basic Independence Exercises (pages 26–27) and practice the written figures on your bass drum, while the rest of the limbs play the basic jazz rhythm part:

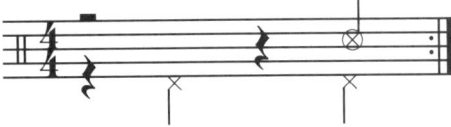

Repeat the same exercises by playing the figures on your hi-hat, while the rest of the limbs play the basic jazz rhythm part:

By playing the patterns using your various limbs, you are further developing your limb control and independence.

Syncopation

Although we have not discussed it yet, many of the examples so far have made use of a technique called *syncopation*. Syncopation means shifting the accent from the downbeats to the upbeats (or skip beats). Syncopation is another important element of jazz drumming because it allows the rhythm to achieve the buoyant feel and forward motion essential to jazz. It helps to think of jazz drumming as a hot potato. When making your drum strokes, mentally think of your stick coming off the drum or rebounding off it. *Feel* the upbeats and syncopation in the music. This is a different approach than playing rock music, where it's all about the downbeats and playing through the drums (in other words, many rock drummers focus on the downward motion of the stick, not the rebound).

Gene Krupa (1909–1973), born in Chicago, Illinois, is best known for his work with Benny Goodman, Teddy Wilson and Lionel Hampton. Krupa's drumming on Goodman's "Sing, Sing, Sing" made him a national celebrity. He made history in 1927 with Eddie Condon's band, when he became the first drummer ever to make a record featuring a full drumset. Krupa worked closely with drum and cymbal manufacturers to develop many standard elements of the modern drumset, such as the bass drum pedal and the hi-hat.

Chapter 4: The Various Styles of Jazz

Now that you've learned the cornerstone of jazz—the swing rhythm—we're going to go over the various styles commonly found within jazz music and its standard repertoire. Throughout its evolution, jazz has absorbed and inspired many new rhythms. As a result, many different types of jazz music have evolved, such as ragtime, Dixieland, big band, fusion, avant-garde, Latin jazz, jazz rock, bebop, smooth jazz and acid jazz. The following is a basic introduction to the various rhythms that you should be familiar with when playing jazz.

Second Line or Street Beat

New Orleans is considered to be the birthplace of jazz and, with its deep musical history, the city has also given birth to some distinctive rhythms. One of those rhythms is *second line*. Second line is a tradition that comes from the famous jazz funerals in New Orleans. The first line consisted of family and friends of the deceased and integral members of the funeral ceremony. The marching bands that led these funeral processions would attract onlookers strictly on the basis of the music they were playing. The people that would join the procession, because they enjoyed the music, became known as the "second line." Hence, the rhythm the marching bands were playing became known as second line or street beat.

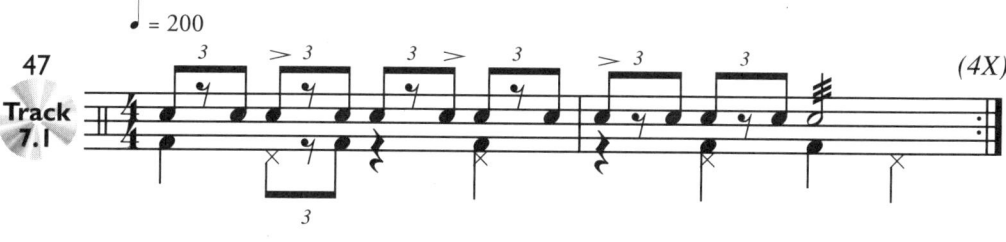

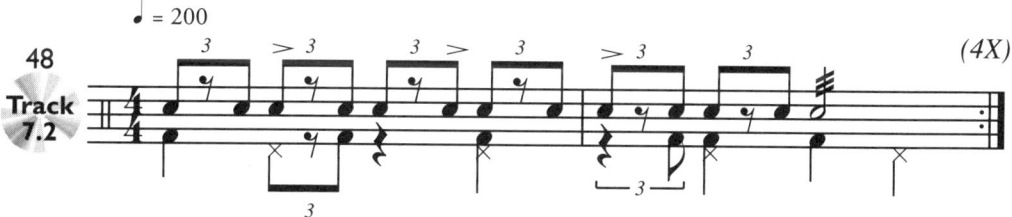

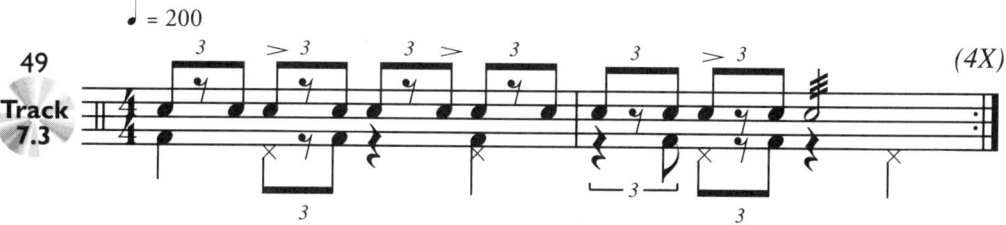

The Jazz Waltz

The *waltz* has its origins in Vienna, Austria in the late eighteenth century. Originally, the waltz was a ballroom dance in 3/4 time. In the early twentieth century, the waltz rhythm was adopted by American musical theater and film composers. Since so many famous jazz standards come from the Tin Pan Alley (a group of publishers and songwriters based in New York City that produced the popular songs of the early twentieth century), particularly show tunes, the adaptation of the waltz in jazz was natural. Some jazz standards that call upon a drummer to play a 3/4 jazz waltz are "All Blues" (Miles Davis), "Up Jumped Spring" (Freddie Hubbard) and "Bluesette" (Toots Thielemans).

A characteristic of the waltz is the accenting of the 2nd and 3rd beats, represented by the hi-hat. Below are some variations on the waltz rhythm.

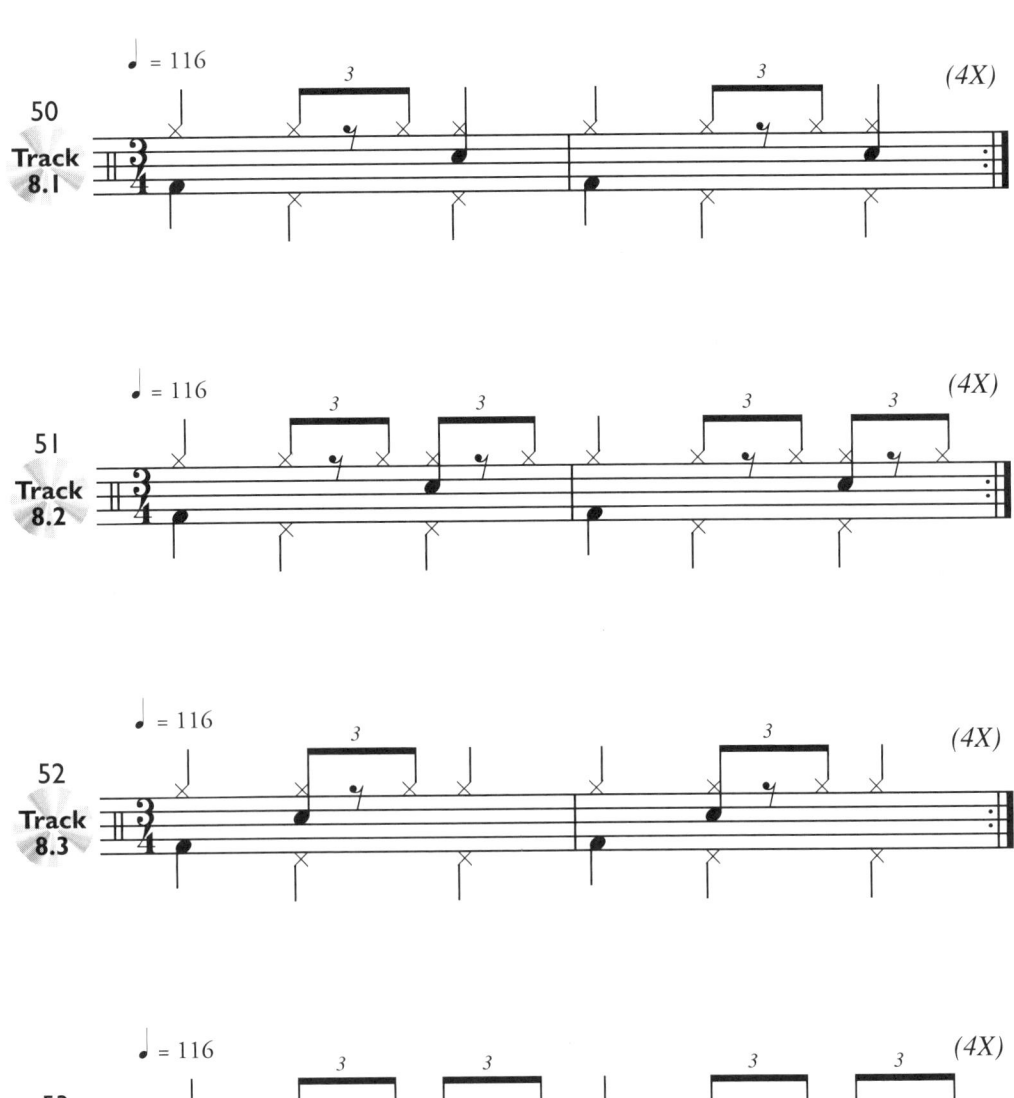

Latin Rhythms

Latin rhythms are very popular within the jazz context. Once used in a very general way, the term "Latin" has been broken down over the years to distinguish between the rhythms of Brazil, Cuba, Puerto Rico and other Caribbean Islands.

Brazilian Rhythms: Bossa Nova and Samba

Brazil is the region from which the rhythms of bossa nova and samba originate. The rhythms you will see in the following exercises are typically played with Brazilian percussion instruments such as the caixa, surdo and tamborim, but we will be emulating these sounds on the drumset. Standard jazz tunes such as "One Note Samba" (Antonio Carlos Jobim), "Blue Bossa" (Kenny Dorham), "Ceora" (Lee Morgan) and "Desafinado" (Jobim) all call for these types of rhythms.

Bossa Nova

Bossa nova is a style of Brazilian music invented in the late 1950s in the Copacabana and Ipanema beachside districts of Rio de Janeiro. The name translates to "the new beat" or "the new way." Antonio Carlos Jobim and João Gilberto are known for popularizing the bossa nova.

The music derives from the samba (see page 32) but is more complex harmonically and less percussive. Following are some examples of the bossa nova rhythm.

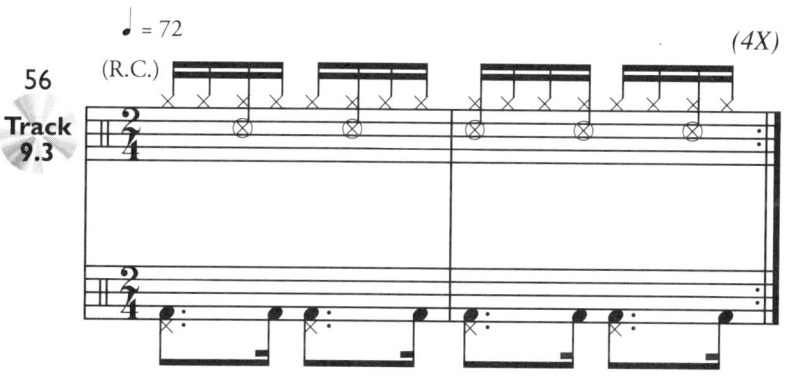

The Total Jazz Drummer 31

Samba

Samba is a quick, highly percussive and syncopated Brazilian carnival dance song that developed as a distinctive kind of music at the beginning of the twentieth century in Rio de Janeiro. It is one of the most famous music forms in Brazil arising from African roots. Check out the CD for slow and up to tempo versions of the following examples.

32 The Total Jazz Drummer

Afro-Cuban Rhythms

Afro-Cuban rhythms come from the Caribbean islands like Cuba, Puerto Rico and Trinidad. Like Brazilian rhythms, they have a strong African influence. They are home to the rhythms of mambo, salsa, songo, bembé, abakwa and calypso. You'll be asked to play these grooves with jazz standards like "A Night in Tunisia" (Dizzy Gillespie), "On Green Dolphin Street" (Bronislau Kaper), "St. Thomas" (Sonny Rollins) and "Con Alma" (Dizzy Gillespie).

Clave

The most popular Afro-Cuban rhythms you will encounter within the jazz context come from Cuba and Puerto Rico. They are salsa and mambo. In order to understand and get the feel of these rhythms, it is vital to understand the importance of *clave*. Clave is a Spanish word that means "key." The clave in these rhythms serves as the skeletal rhythmic figure around which the different drums and percussion instruments are played (Note: *Claves* are also two wooden sticks that are used to play the clave pattern).

There are four clave patterns with which you should be familiar.

3-2 Son Clave

3-2 indicates that there are 3 notes in the first bar and 2 notes in the second bar. The first bar is called the 3-part of the clave and the second bar is called the 2-part of the clave.

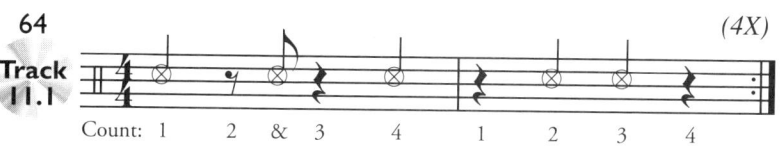

2-3 Son Clave

This is simply the reverse of the 3-2 pattern.

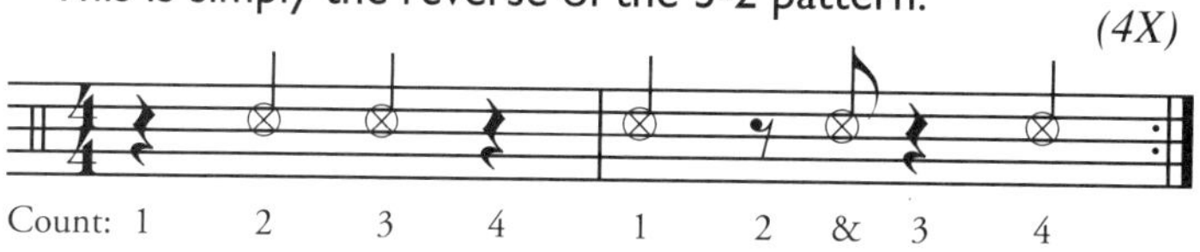

3-2 Rumba Clave

Rumba clave delays the 3rd note by one eighth note.

2-3 Rumba Clave

Again, this is the reverse of the 3-2 pattern.

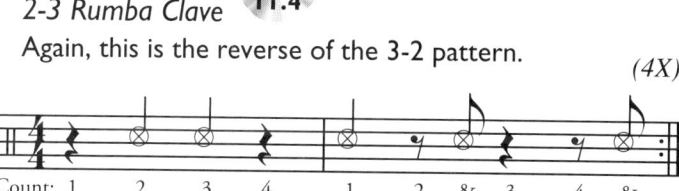

The Total Jazz Drummer   33

Now that you understand what clave is, let's put it into context with the overall sound of these rhythms. The rhythms you will see in the following exercises are typically played with instruments such as congas, claves, timbales, bongos, maracas and cowbell, but we will be emulating these sounds on the drumset.

Mambo

The mambo, made popular in Cuba in the latter half of the 1930s, is a musical form and dance. The cymbal pattern, typically played on a *mambo bell* (a wide, low-pitched bell), is what characteristically defines this rhythm.

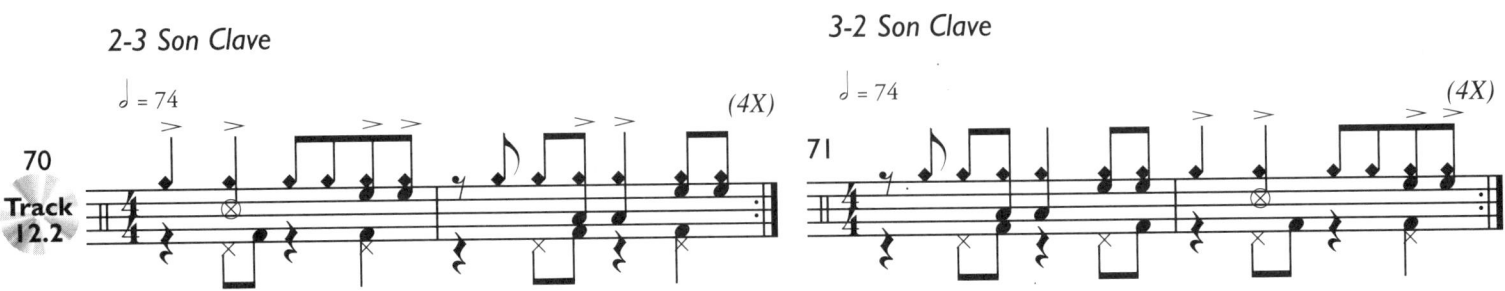

The next two examples utilize the toms in order to imitate the sound of the congas.

34   The Total Jazz Drummer

Salsa

Salsa is essentially Cuban in stylistic origin; however, it was developed in New York City in the 1960s by Cuban and Puerto Rican immigrants. Although similar to the feel of the mambo, what distinguishes salsa from mambo is the *cáscara* (shell) pattern played on the side of the timbales. In these examples, the cáscara pattern is played on the ride cymbal; you could also play it on the side or rim of the floor tom in order to imitate the sound of the timbales.

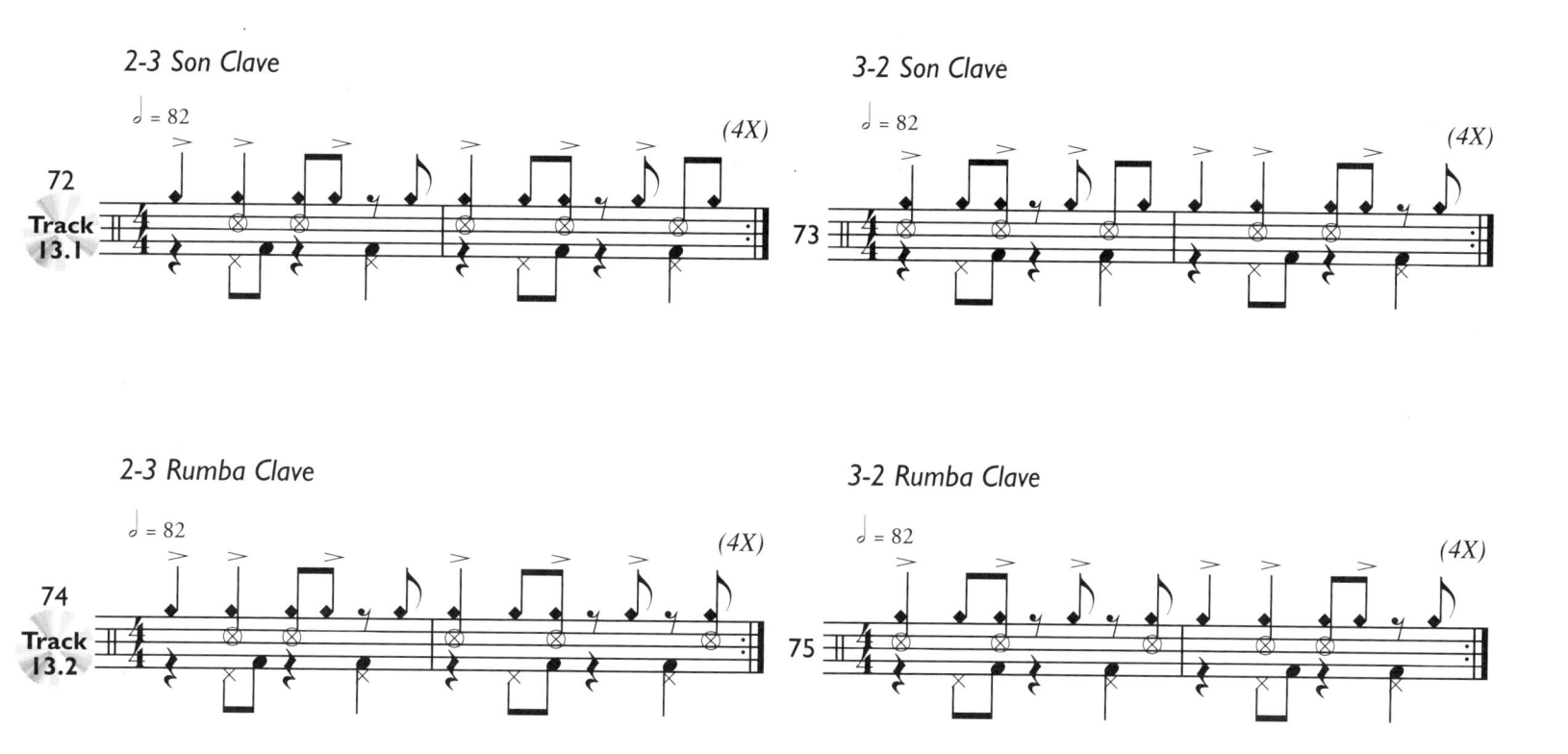

2-3 Son Clave

3-2 Son Clave

2-3 Rumba Clave

3-2 Rumba Clave

The next two examples utilize the toms in order to imitate the sound of the congas.

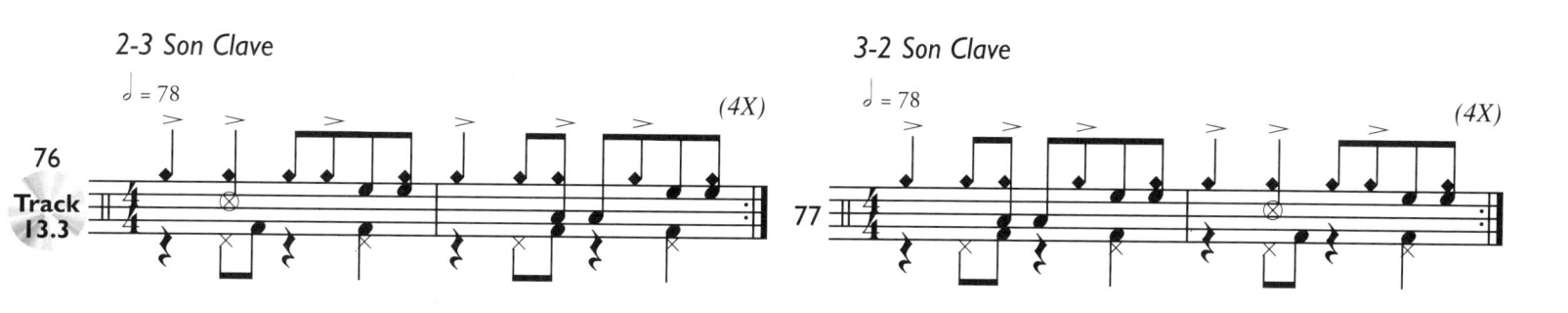

2-3 Son Clave

3-2 Son Clave

The Total Jazz Drummer

Songo

Songo is one of the few Latin rhythms actually created for the drumset in the early 1970s. The great percussionist Changuito of the Cuban group Los Van Van is recognized as the creator of this rhythm. The songo is different from other Latin rhythms in that the cymbal pattern maintains a very basic half-note pattern, while the left hand is filling in the gaps on the drums. Notice also how the bass drum is consistently hitting the "&" of beat 2. This syncopation gives the rhythm a driving feel. Listen to slow and up-to-tempo versions of the following two examples on the CD.

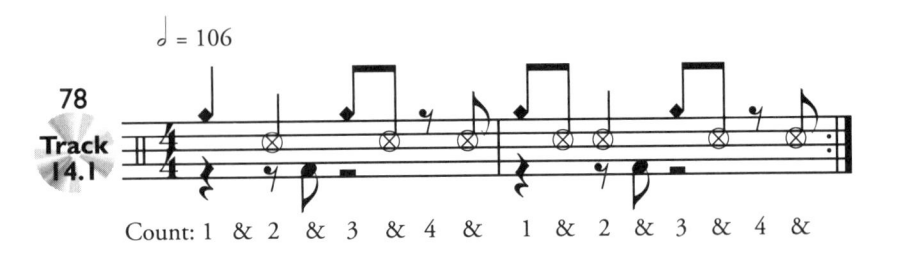

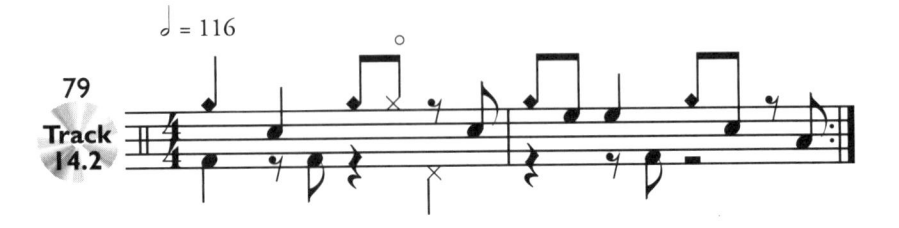

Count: 1 & 2 & 3 & 4 &   1 & 2 & 3 & 4 &

Below are some more variations for you to try.

Watch for the roll in the first bar of the following example.

36   The Total Jazz Drummer

Bembé

Bembé is a popular $^6_8$ rhythm from Cuba and is named after a type of religious drumming party. Its origins are West African; some of the fundamental rhythms that come from there are based on $^6_8$ and $^{12}_8$ feels. The exercises will be written in both $^6_8$ and $^4_4$ time so you can get used to seeing the same rhythms written differently.

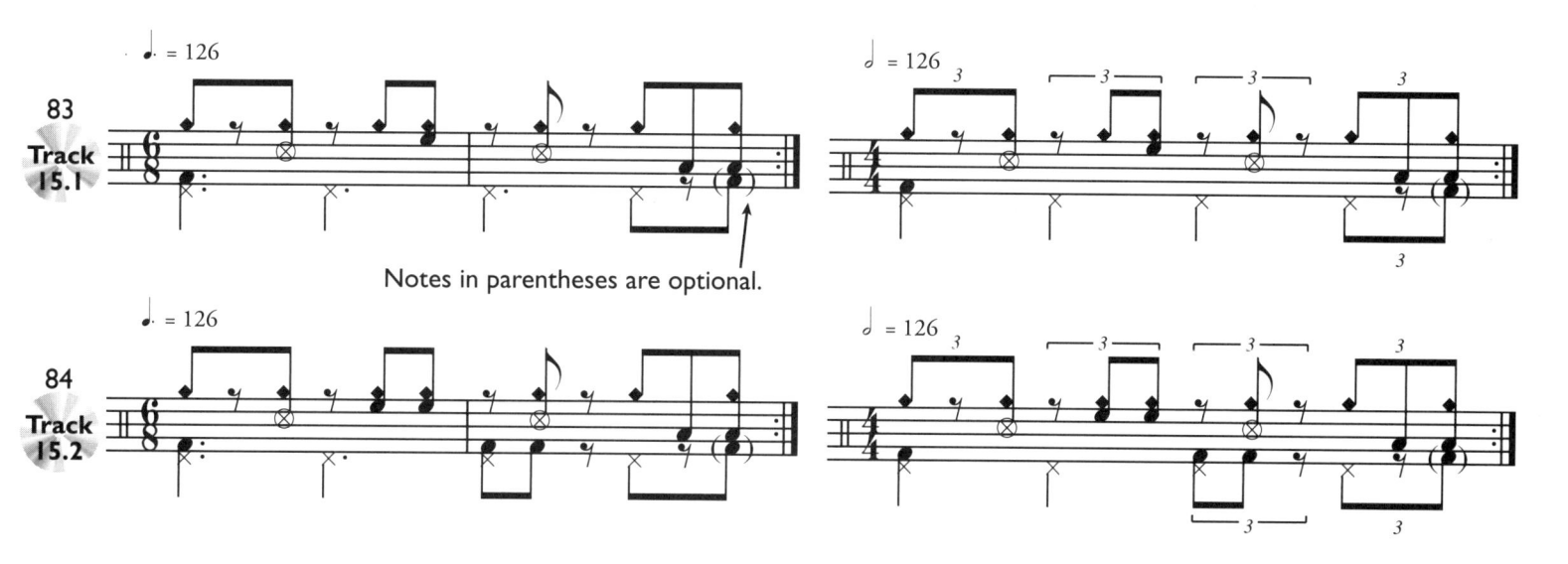

Notes in parentheses are optional.

Abakwa

Another $^6_8$ feel of Cuba is the *Abakwa* (or Abakuá), which is named for a secret society with roots from Nigeria and Cameroon. This is a noteworthy $^6_8$ pattern because of the feel generated from the "4 against 3" *polyrhythm*. (A polyrhythm is two or more different rhythms played simultaneously. We'll get more into polyrhythmic exercises later in the book). Again, this exercise will be written in both $^6_8$ time and $^4_4$ time.

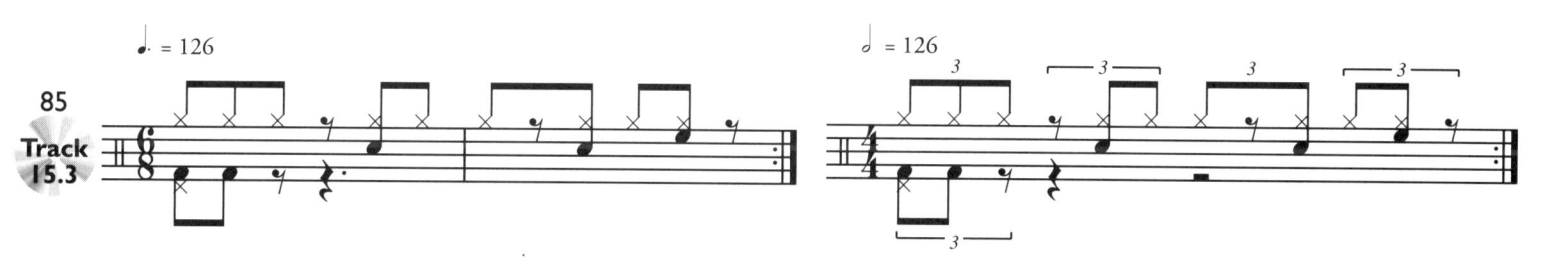

The Total Jazz Drummer 37

Calypso

Calypso is a style of music that originated at the beginning of the twentieth century, primarily on the island of Trinidad. The bass drum and hi-hat play a consistent pattern while the interplay between the toms creates a type of melody. Calypso is the predecessor to reggae, soca and the now popular reggaeton.

Straight Eighths

In jazz, you'll often encounter songs that require the drummer to play a *straight eighths* groove. There is a variety of straight eighths feels, such as funk, rhythm and blues (R&B), soul, rock, fusion, boogaloo (a fusion of R&B and Cuban music that was popular in the U.S. from 1966–1969) and ECM (a style of playing identified with a jazz record label of the same name). Many grooves can cross over from style to style, but what differentiates them is the feel you use when playing them. A funk groove requires a different touch and approach compared to a rock groove. The same goes for R&B to fusion, but you'll still find many of the same rhythms being used from style to style. Be sure to check out these masters of the straight-eighth groove: Clyde Stubblefield (James Brown), Al Jackson (Al Green, Donny Hathaway), Bernard Purdie (Aretha Frankin, B.B. King), Dave Garibaldi (Tower of Power), Steve Gadd (Steely Dan, Paul Simon), Harvey Mason (Herbie Hancock) and Jack DeJohnette (Keith Jarrett). Here are some examples to get you familiar with straight eighth grooves. Practice these rhythms both on the ride cymbal and on the hi-hat and at varying tempos.

Examples 90–92 are in the ECM style.

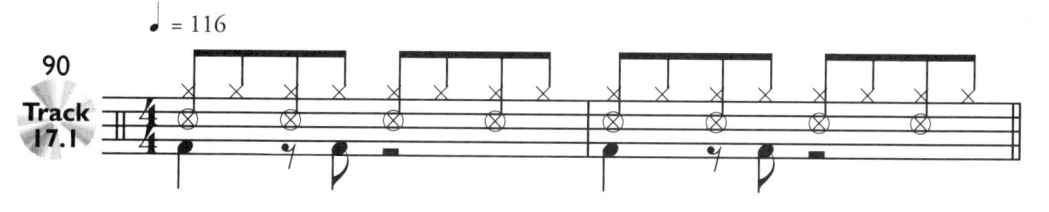

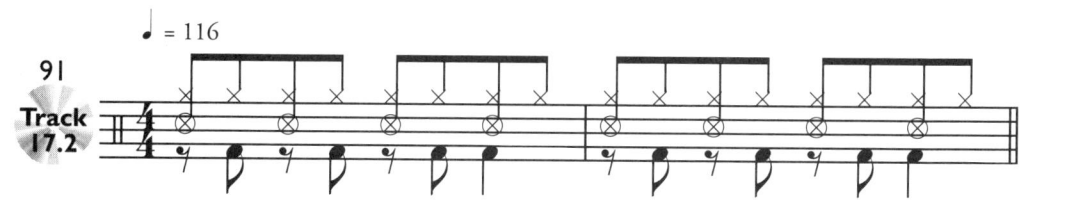

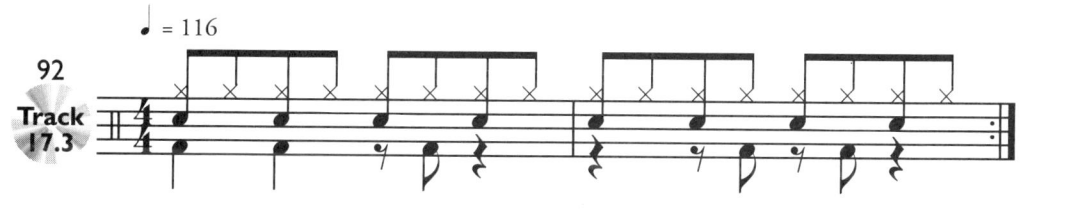

Here is an example in the boogaloo style.

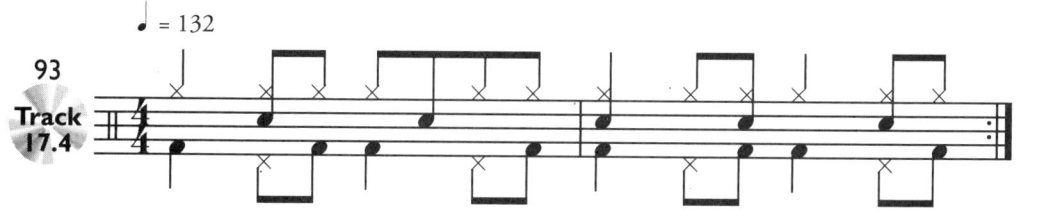

The Total Jazz Drummer 39

The next four pages are filled with straight eighth grooves for you to practice.

The Total Jazz Drummer 41

112
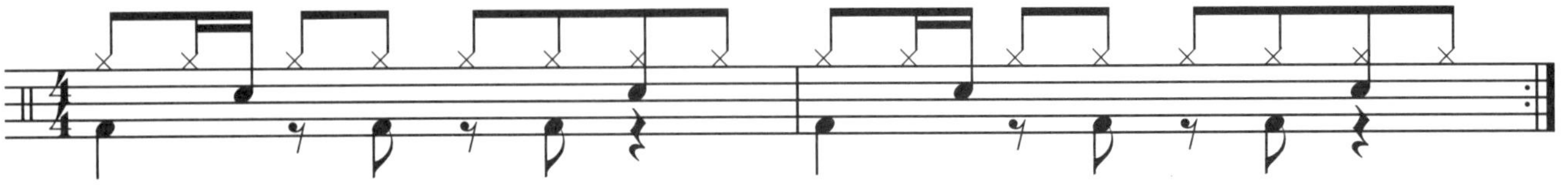

113
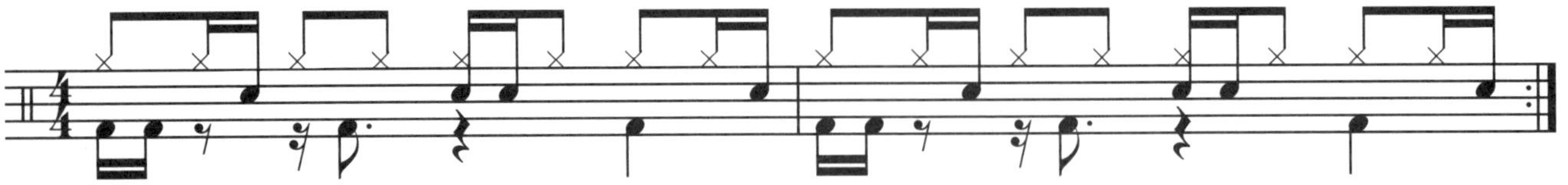

114
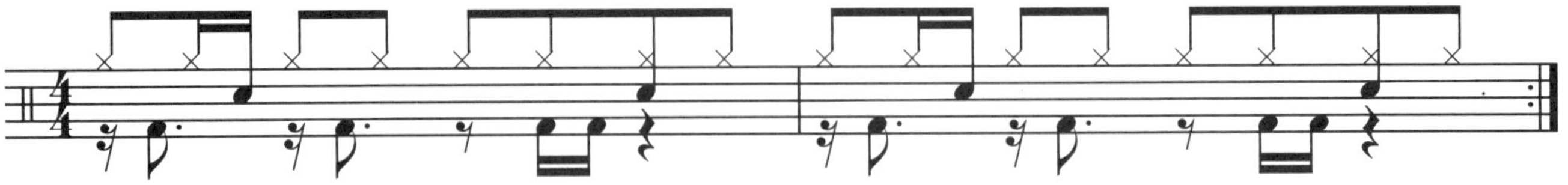

115
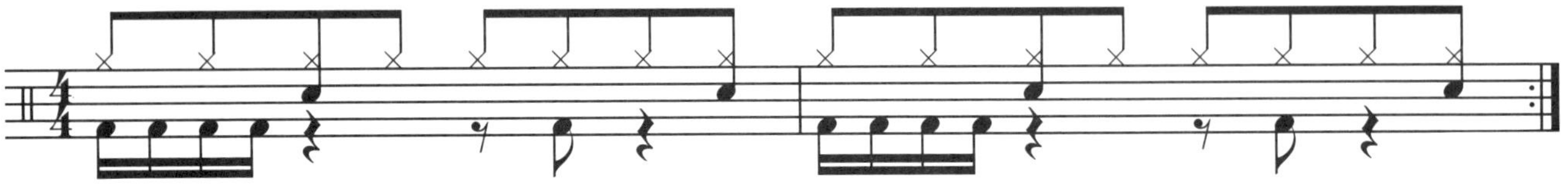

116
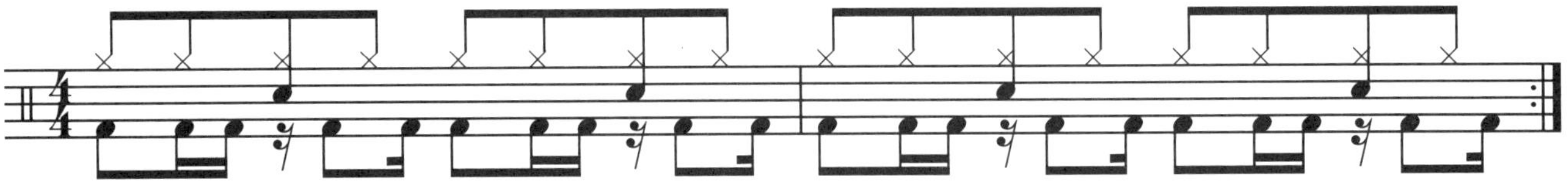

117
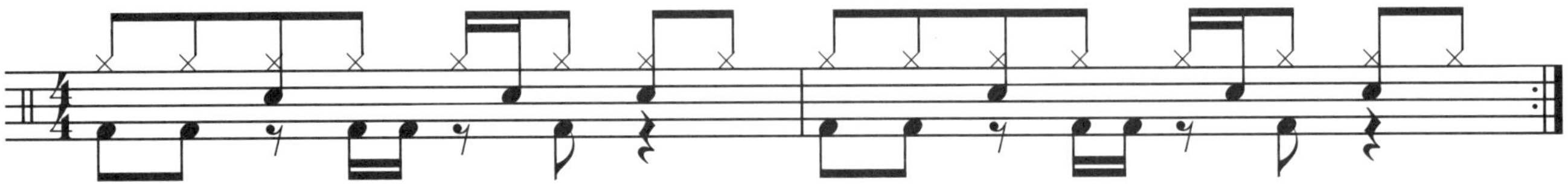

118
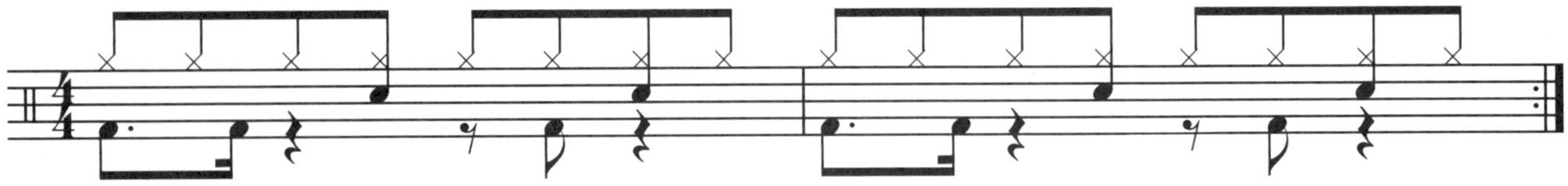

119
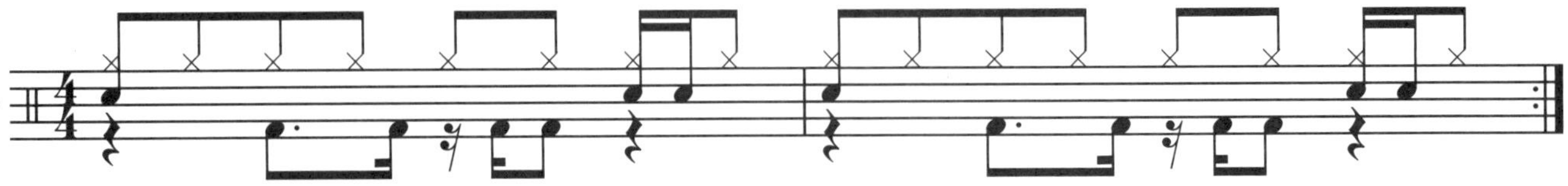

120
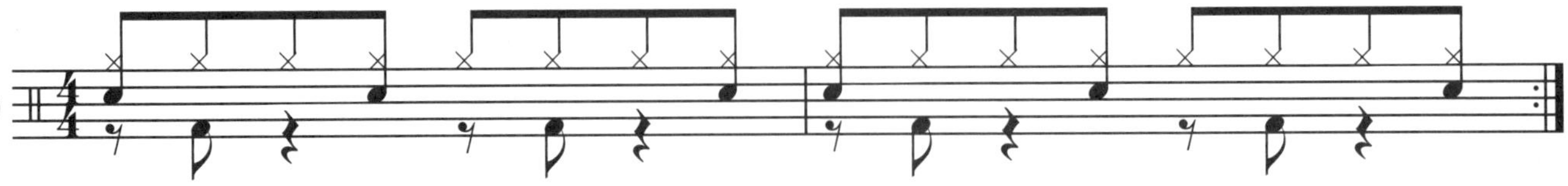

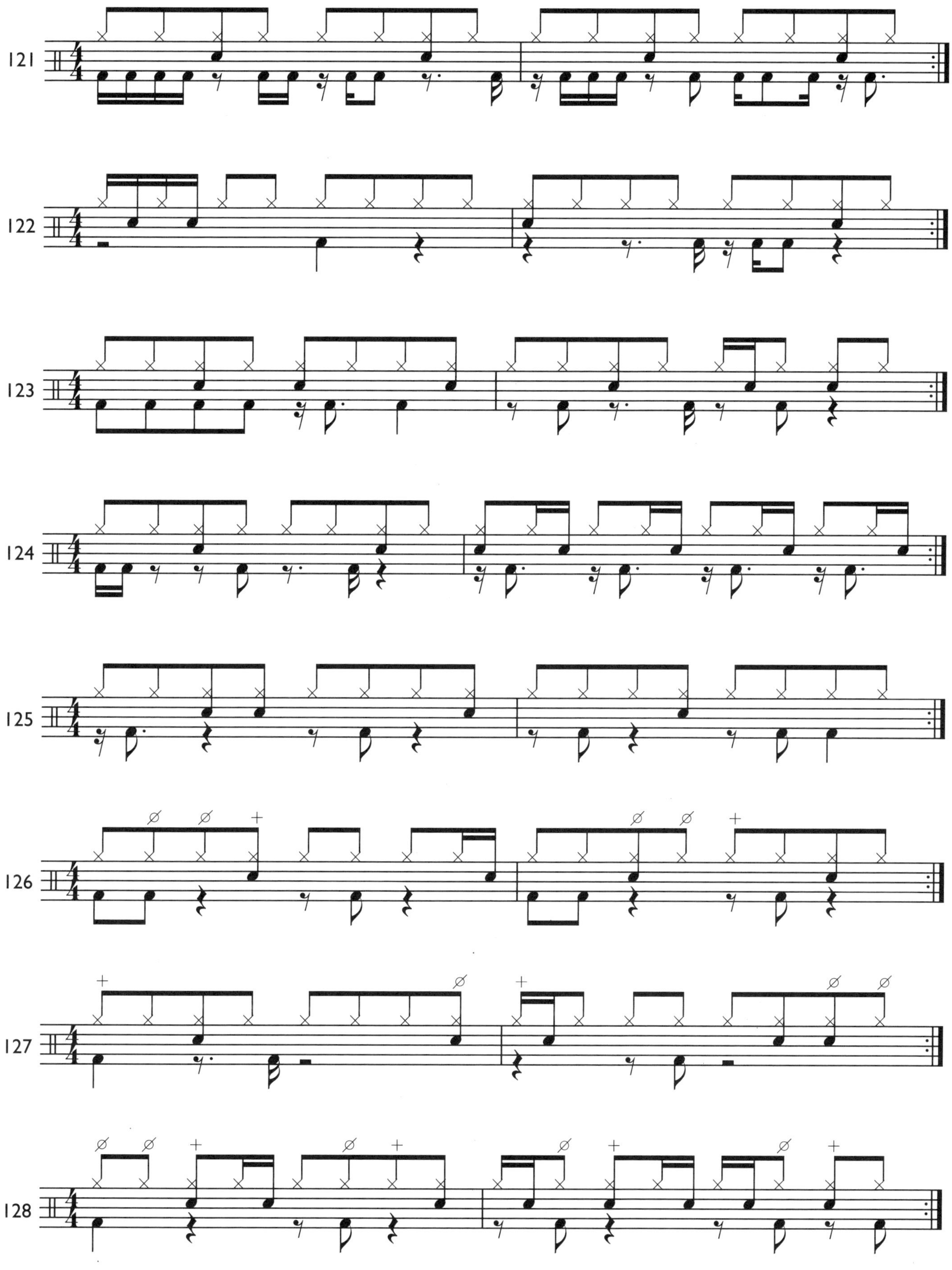
121
122
123
124
125
126
127
128

Straight Eighth Cymbal Patterns

For advanced study, once you get used to the rhythms on the previous five pages, you can apply a variety of hi-hat or ride cymbal patterns like the ones below. Play the accents as written on a partially open hi-hat or on the bell of your ride cymbal.

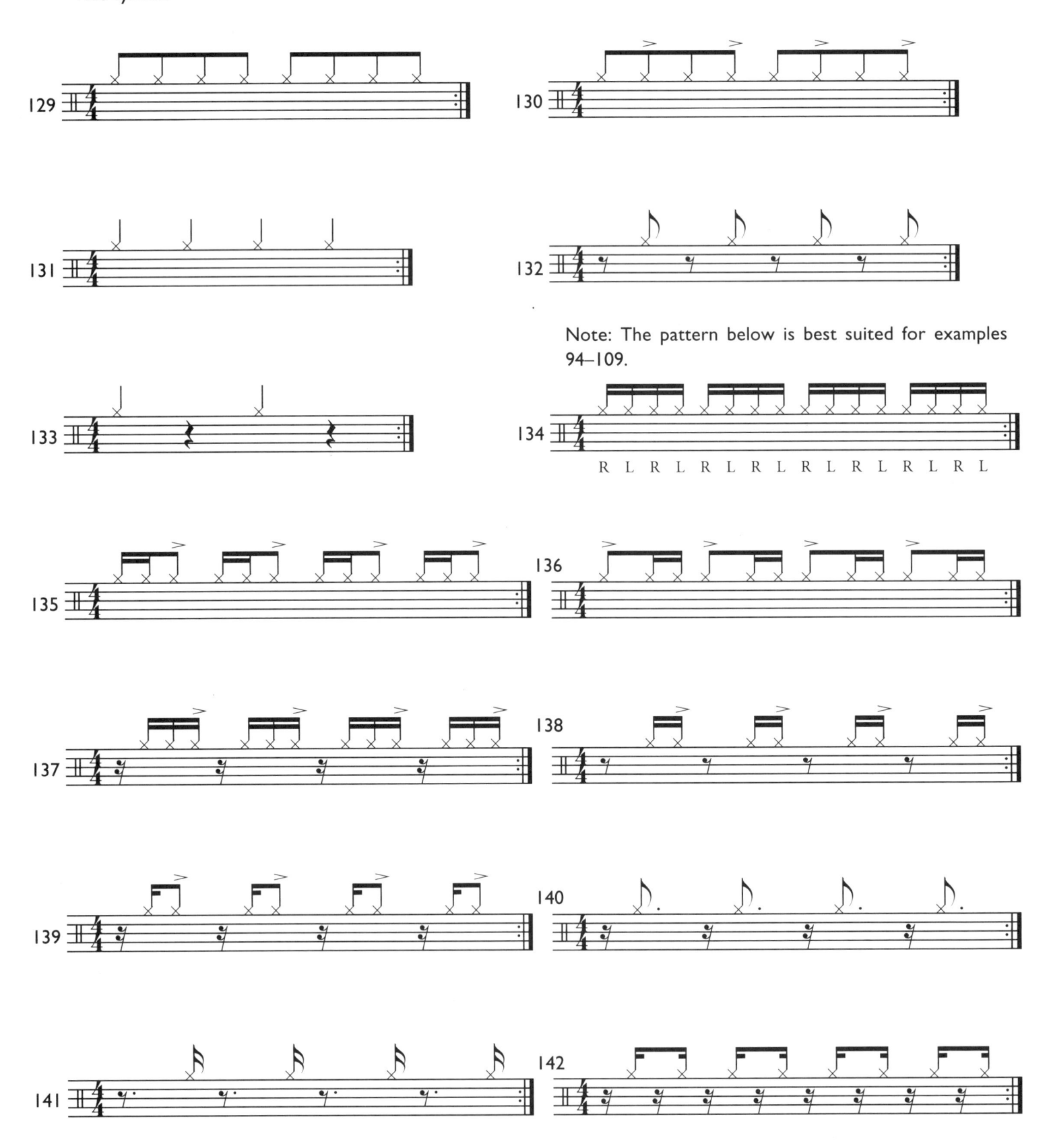

Note: The pattern below is best suited for examples 94–109.

R L R L R L R L R L R L R L R L

PART 2: The Intermediate Jazz Drummer

Welcome to Part 2. At this point, you've learned the fundamental rhythms of jazz drumming. We're now going to delve deeper into the jazz drumming vocabulary by developing your coordination skills and internal pulse, learning the styles of a few key jazz drumming pioneers and getting into the art of brush playing.

Practicing

Before we carry on, I'd like to make some suggestions to add on to your practice routine from Part 1 of this book:

- Go back and review all the practice suggestions from Part 1 (see page 6).

- Practice along to recordings of the jazz drummers we will be going over in this section: "Papa" Jo Jones, "Philly" Joe Jones, Max Roach, Elvin Jones and Tony Williams.

- Increase your practice time to a minimum of one hour a day, seven days week. The more you practice, the better chance you'll have of absorbing this material.

- Listen to all the pivotal jazz recordings. Please refer to the Listening Guide at the end of this book for a start (see page 124).

- Remember, practicing means working on the things you cannot yet play on the drumset, not jamming on all the stuff you can play.

- Be open to improvising and/or building your own ideas on any of the exercises. Doing this strengthens your creativity, your personal style and your ability to improvise.

Chapter 5: The Art of Brushes

Using the brushes.

Brushes are a type of drumstick with bristles at the end. The bristles can be made of wire or plastic, and the base of the stick is usually wood or rubber. They somewhat resemble a miniature broom. Playing with brushes is a unique part of jazz drumming and should be approached as an art unto itself. There is a variety of sounds that you can only get using brushes; these sounds will greatly enhance your drumming vocabulary.

First, hold the brushes as you would hold your sticks. Now, before jumping right into the techniques and patterns laid out in this book, you should take a moment to play with your brushes. Explore the different sounds you can get by playing your brushes in various ways. You can play with the tip of the brushes, or depending upon how much pressure you apply with the brushes against the drum head, you can have varying degrees of the body of the brush playing on the drum head. You can slide the brush across the drum head, lightly tap it or slap the brush on the head. Playing the brushes is similar to martial arts, painting or swimming; it's all about having a fluid movement. The sounds and rhythms you get from the drum are dependent upon the graceful motion of your arms, wrists, hands and fingers.

Brush Strokes

On page 47 are five basic brush strokes that give you different sounds.

Here are a few suggestions for practicing these strokes:

- Practice the movement with just your hands and no brushes.

- Practice with each hand separately and then together.

- Practice very slowly.

- Practice playing along with albums by the brush masters such as "Papa" Jo Jones and "Philly" Joe Jones.

- Practice applying varying degrees of the brush to the drum head, from just the tip to the full body of the brush.

- Practice producing *closed* sounds by striking the drum and keeping the brush on it to mute the sound. Then, practice *open* sounds by striking the drum and quickly retracting the brush so the sound can ring out.

143
Tap — Track 18

The *tap* stroke uses only the tips of the brushes to create a light sound. It is your most basic stroke. It is similar to playing with your sticks, except that you don't get much of a rebound from the head. You must involve your wrists and fingers more to bring the brushes back off the head after striking the drum. You should practice your drum rudiments with brushes using only the taps. This will build strength and speed in your fingers and hands. Listen to the example on the CD.

144
Swish — Track 19

The *swish* sound is what makes the brushes unique. The brush stays on the head the entire time, moving either from side to side or in a circular motion. The goal is to create a consistent, sustained sound in which you can still hear the inherent rhythm. The arm motion is similar to stirring a big pot of stew. Listen to the example on the CD.

145
Slap — Track 20

The *slap* is similar to the tap technique, however, you use the whole body of the brush to get a full sound.

146
Sweep — Track 21

The *sweep* can be accomplished in the same manner as the swish, except that you pick up the brush from the drum head at the end of your stroke. The motion is literally like sweeping dirt into a dust pan.

147
Bounce — Track 22

The *bounce* is one of the more difficult techniques, performed by hitting the handle part of the brush against the rim of the drum at a 30 degree angle. At the moment of impact, as the handle of the brush comes to rest against the rim of the drum, the wires of the brushes will start to flutter back and forth very rapidly. You then decrease the angle of the brush so that the wires flutter back and forth against the drum head. This all happens in a matter of seconds. You control how many bounces the brushes make against the drum.

Brush Patterns

Now, when you combine the various brush strokes with one another, you come up with brush patterns. You should experiment with these strokes to come up with patterns of your own. However, the following pages contain some patterns in the styles of two of the greatest brush players in the history of jazz: "Papa" Jo Jones and "Philly" Joe Jones.

"Papa" Jo Jones (1911–1985) was one of the most influential drummers in jazz history. He was among the first jazz drummers to make the cymbal the primary time keeper, rather than the bass drum, and utilized the drums as a way of punctuating or comping behind a soloist. He played with Art Tatum, Billie Holiday, Lester Young and a host of others, but he is best known for his longstanding association with pianist Count Basie in the 1930s and '40s. He was one of the most brilliant brush players in the history of jazz. Check out Jones's brush solo on "Old Man River" on the album Jo Jones Trio. *It is one of the greatest brush solos in the history of jazz.*

"Philly" Joe Jones (1923–1985, no relation to Jo Jones) was a tremendously influential drummer who swung harder than most. He advanced the jazz drumming vocabulary by taking the bass drum out of its traditional support role and using it as just another drum during his solos. He played with the likes of Tadd Dameron and many others before becoming part of the legendary Miles Davis quintet of the 1950s. There are some great Prestige recordings with this group showcasing "Philly" Joe's amazing musicality on the drums. Check out "Billy Boy" on Miles Davis's album Milestones *for some incredible brush playing.*

48 The Total Jazz Drummer

Nine Basic Brush Patterns

The following pages contain nine basic brush patterns played on the snare drum with your snares off. In order to understand how to play these patterns, refer to the brush legend, which will define the strokes and movement of your brushes in each pattern. Also, be sure to check out "How to Read the Patterns" (below), as this will help you understand each new pattern. It will take time for these patterns to feel comfortable, but as you keep practicing them, your movements will become graceful and fluid. Again, brushes are very different from sticks and require a different touch.

Brush Legend

.	=	*Dot*. Represent taps and are part of notes indicating what rhythm to play.
———	=	*Solid line*. Swish.
- - - - -	=	*Dashed line*. Take brush off drum.
⟶	=	*Arrow*. Indicate direction your brush should follow.
1, 2, 3, 4	=	*Numbers*. Indicate the beat.

How to Read the Patterns

Each brush pattern is notated LH (left hand) RH (right hand). Position your brushes on your snare drum at number 1, the first beat of the rhythm. Now, follow the direction of the arrows to beat 2 and notice if the line is solid (play brush on drum) or dashed (take brush off drum), or if there are just dots (brush just plays rhythm without moving). Continue in the same manner to beat 3 and then beat 4 (in the case of the waltz, only to beat 3). When you arrive at beat 1 again—the beginning of your rhythm—repeat the exercise. On the CD, you will hear four measures of each pattern.

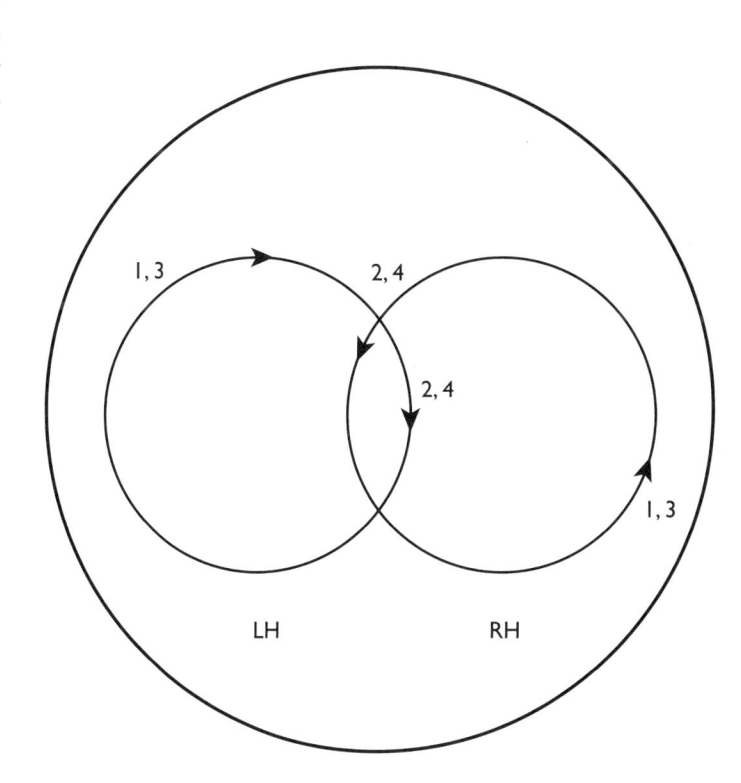

148
Track 23 $\frac{4}{4}$ **Jazz Ballad**

♩ = 60

The Total Jazz Drummer

149 Track 24 — 4/4 **Jazz Ballad** ♩ = 60

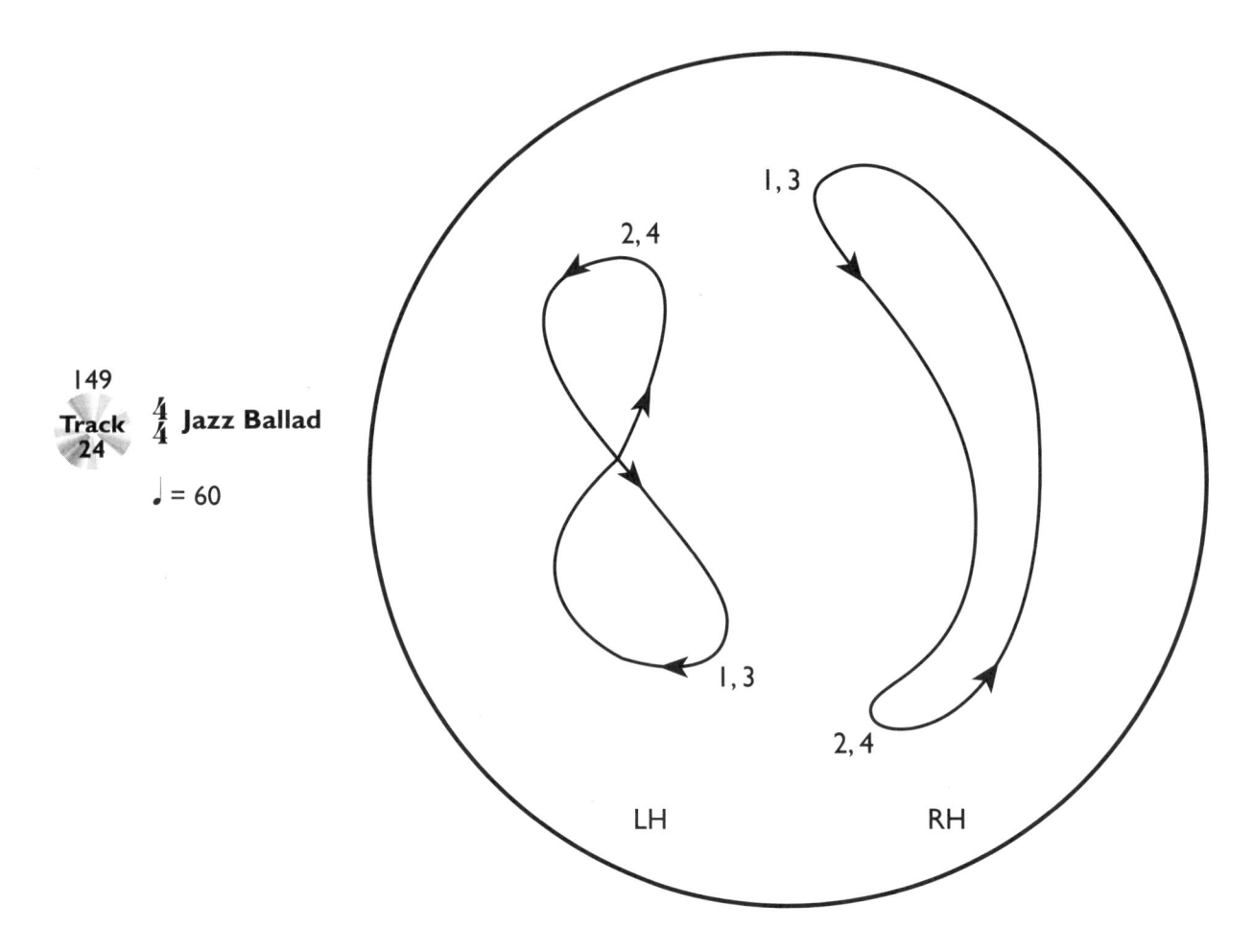

In the example below, note that the right hand has a rhythmic pattern to tap out while the left hand executes its circular pattern.

150 Track 25 — 4/4 **Swing** ♩ = 132

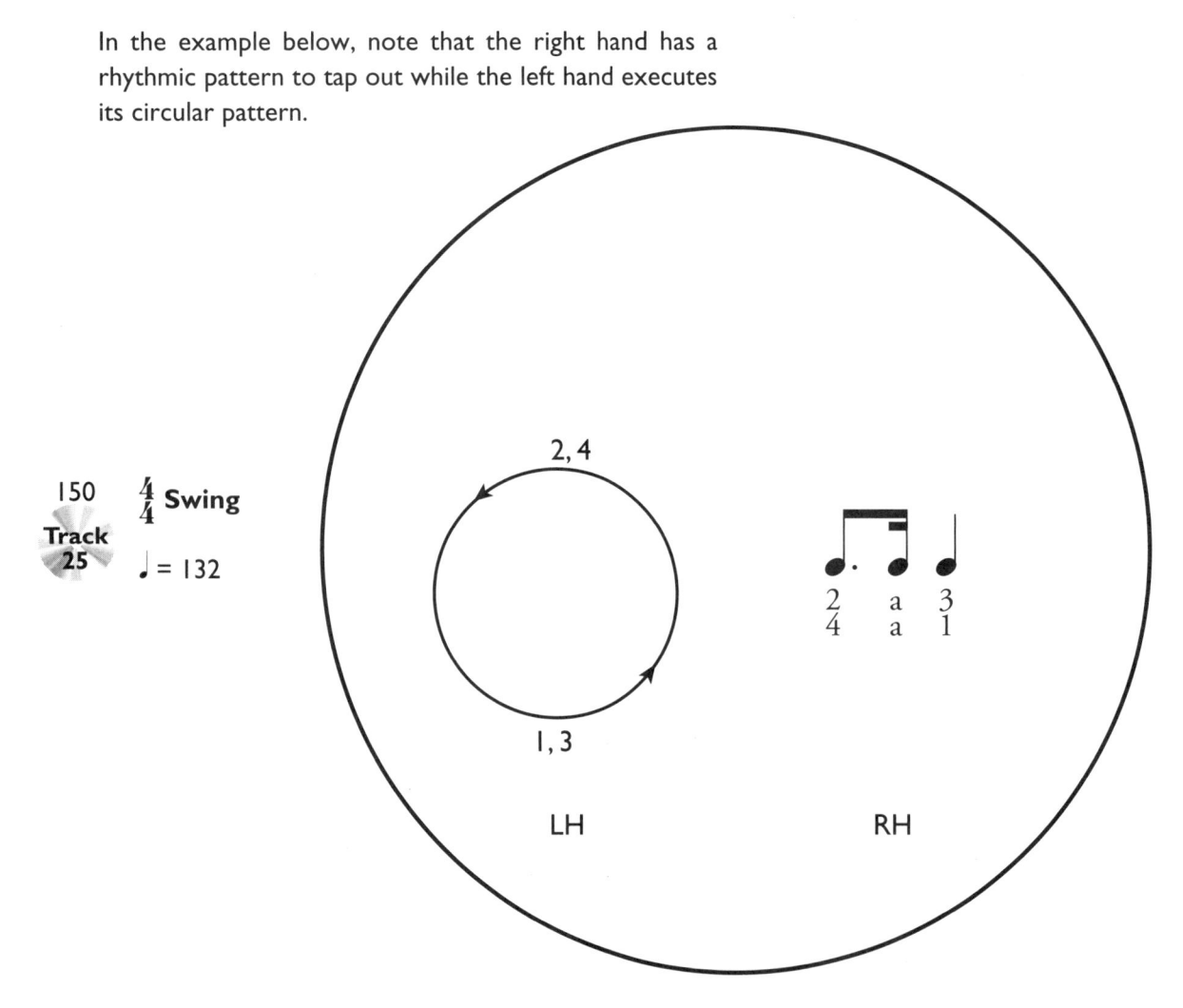

50 The Total Jazz Drummer

The Total Jazz Drummer 51

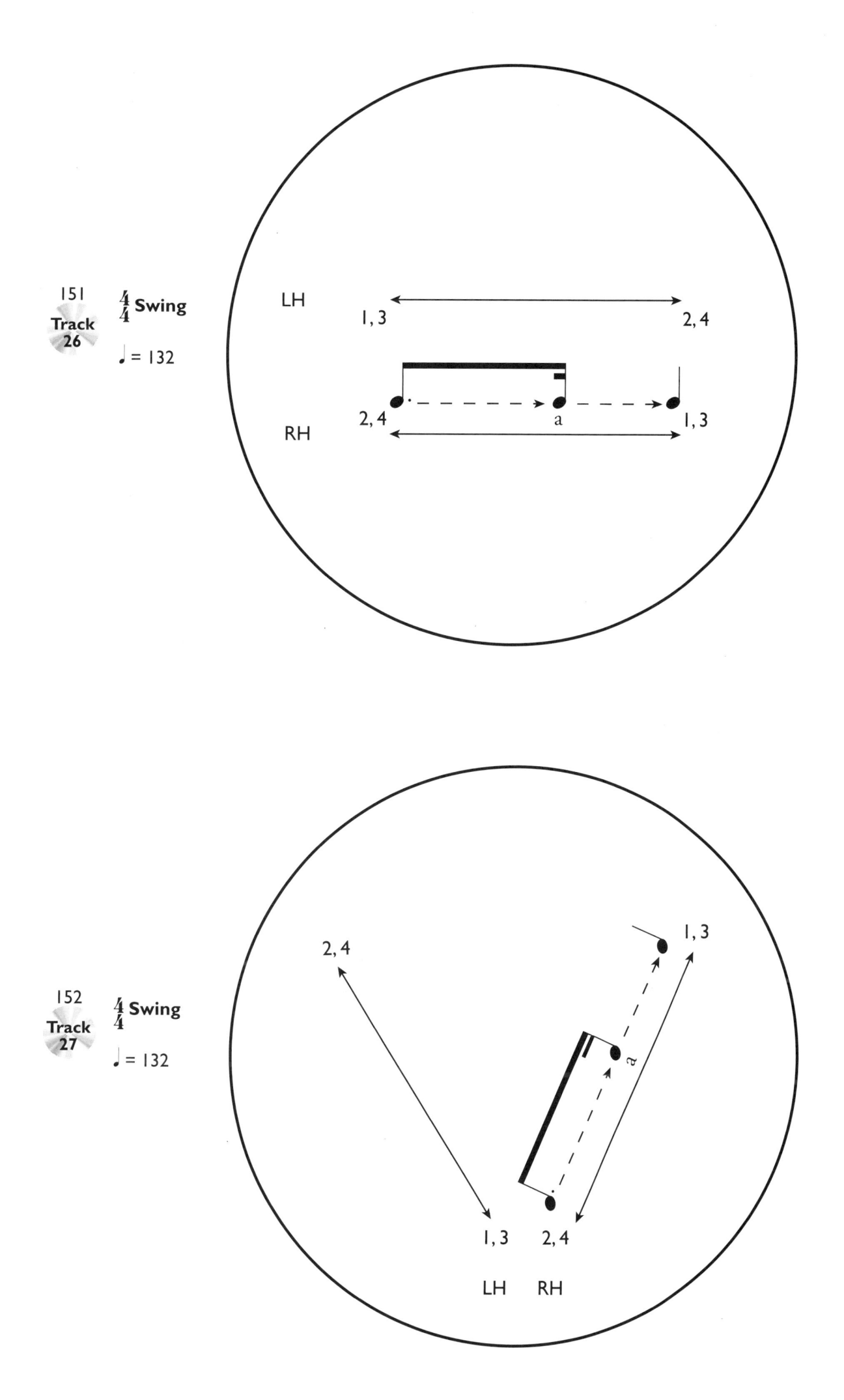

153 $\frac{4}{4}$ **Swing** Track 28   ♩ = 132

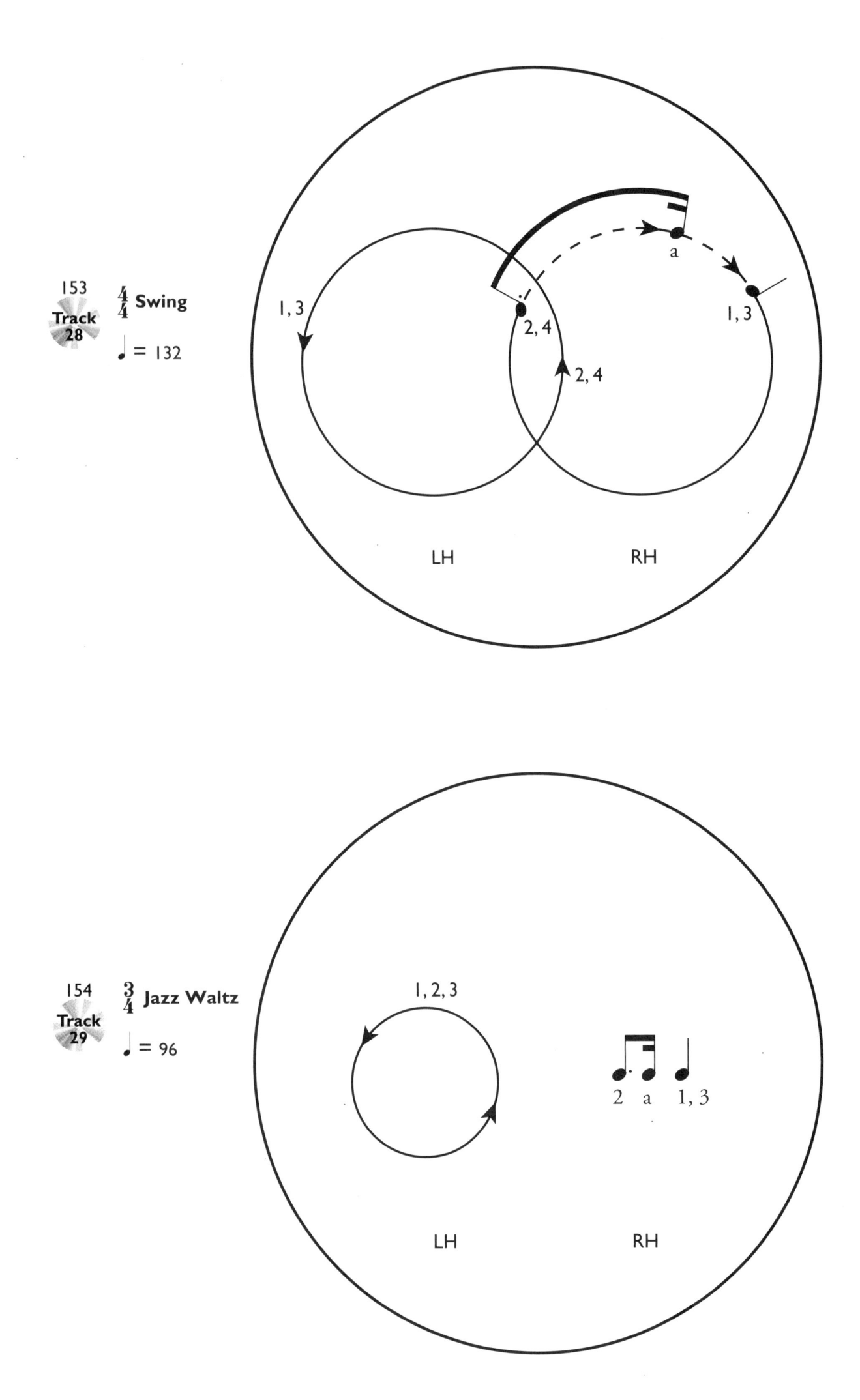

154 $\frac{3}{4}$ **Jazz Waltz** Track 29   ♩ = 96

52 The Total Jazz Drummer

155 **3/4 Jazz Waltz**
Track 30   ♩ = 96

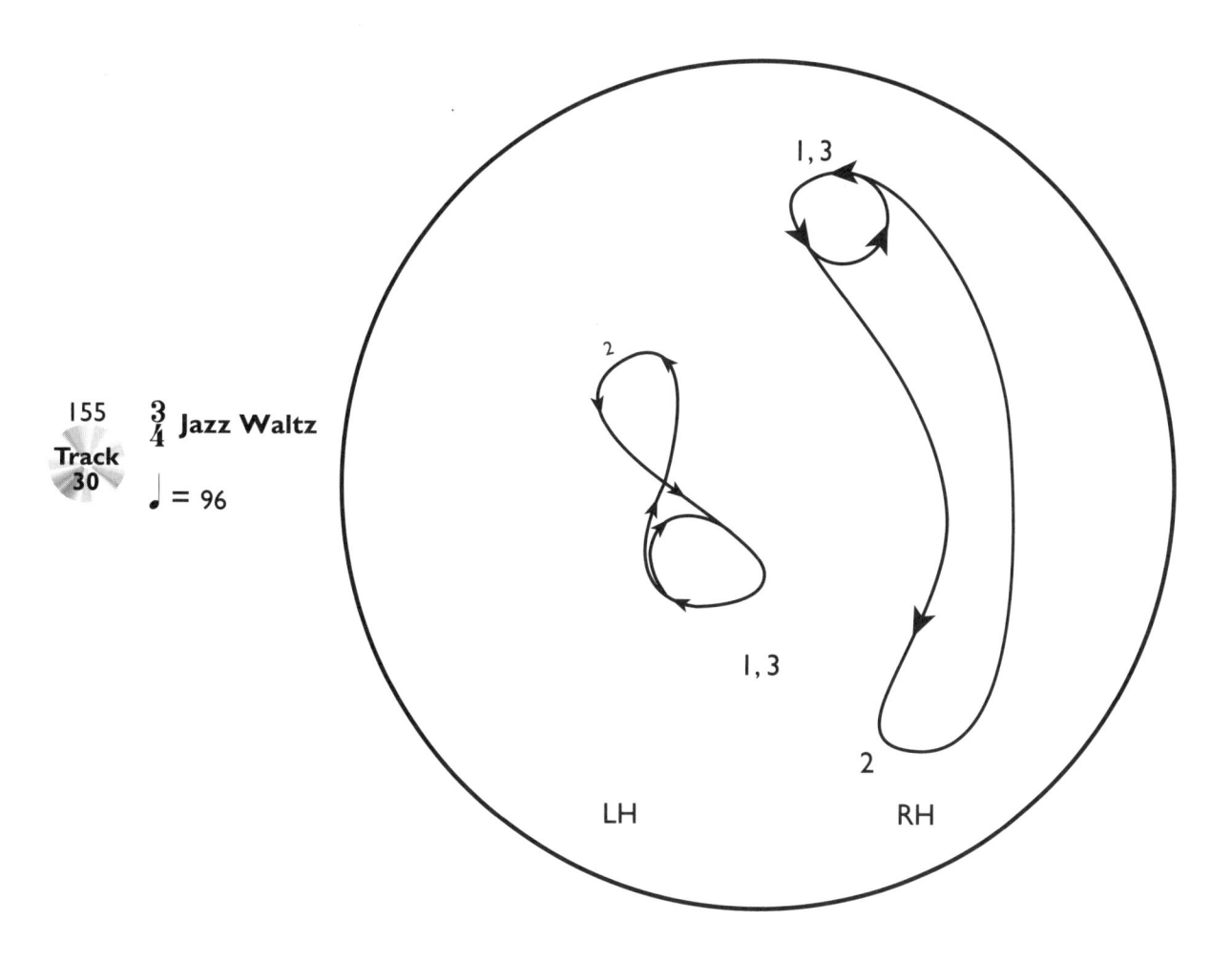

1, 3

2

1, 3

2

LH   RH

156 **4/4 Up Tempo Swing**
Track 31   ♩ = 260

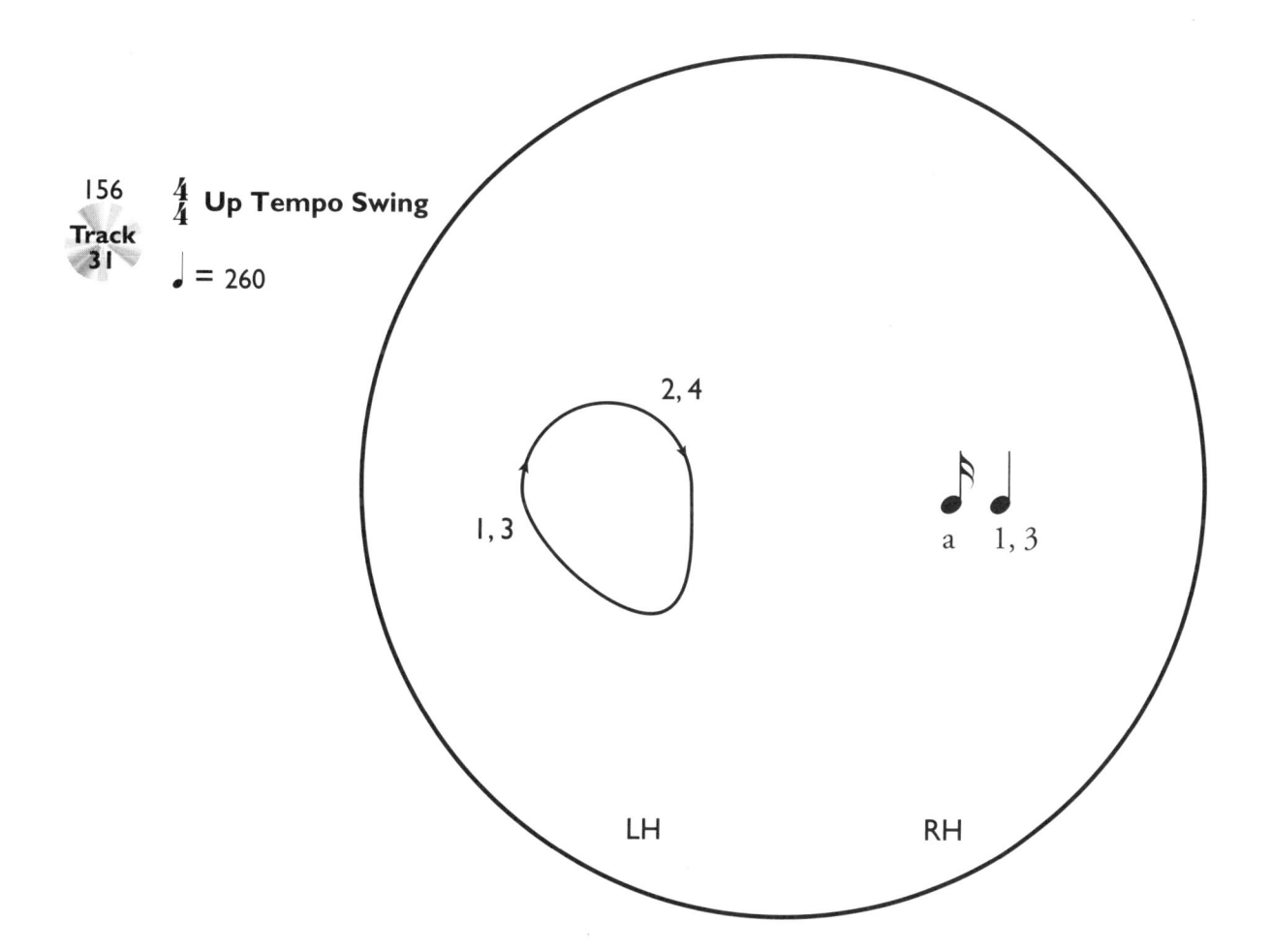

2, 4

1, 3

a   1, 3

LH   RH

The Total Jazz Drummer   53

Chapter 6: Playing Tempos

Different Tempos

Playing at different tempos is crucial for a successful drummer, and the truth is that it's just as hard to play slow as it is fast. In fact, playing slow and playing fast are really the same thing. How is that possible? Well, when you're playing fast, your goal is to subdivide the music into longer phrases so that your body can feel the pulse at a slower tempo. At a fast tempo, trying to count each beat can create a feeling of anxiousness and won't sound relaxed.

You might sound like you're struggling to play fast. If you learn how to think in longer phrases, playing fast becomes much easier. For example, instead of counting an up-tempo swing pattern on each quarter note, try counting just the half notes or even whole notes. Changing the way you count can give the fast tempo a "jazzy" loping feel, as the following examples demonstrate.

Count up tempo on quarters (1, 2, 3, 4), half notes (1,3), whole notes (1,1), etc. and play ride cymbal pattern.

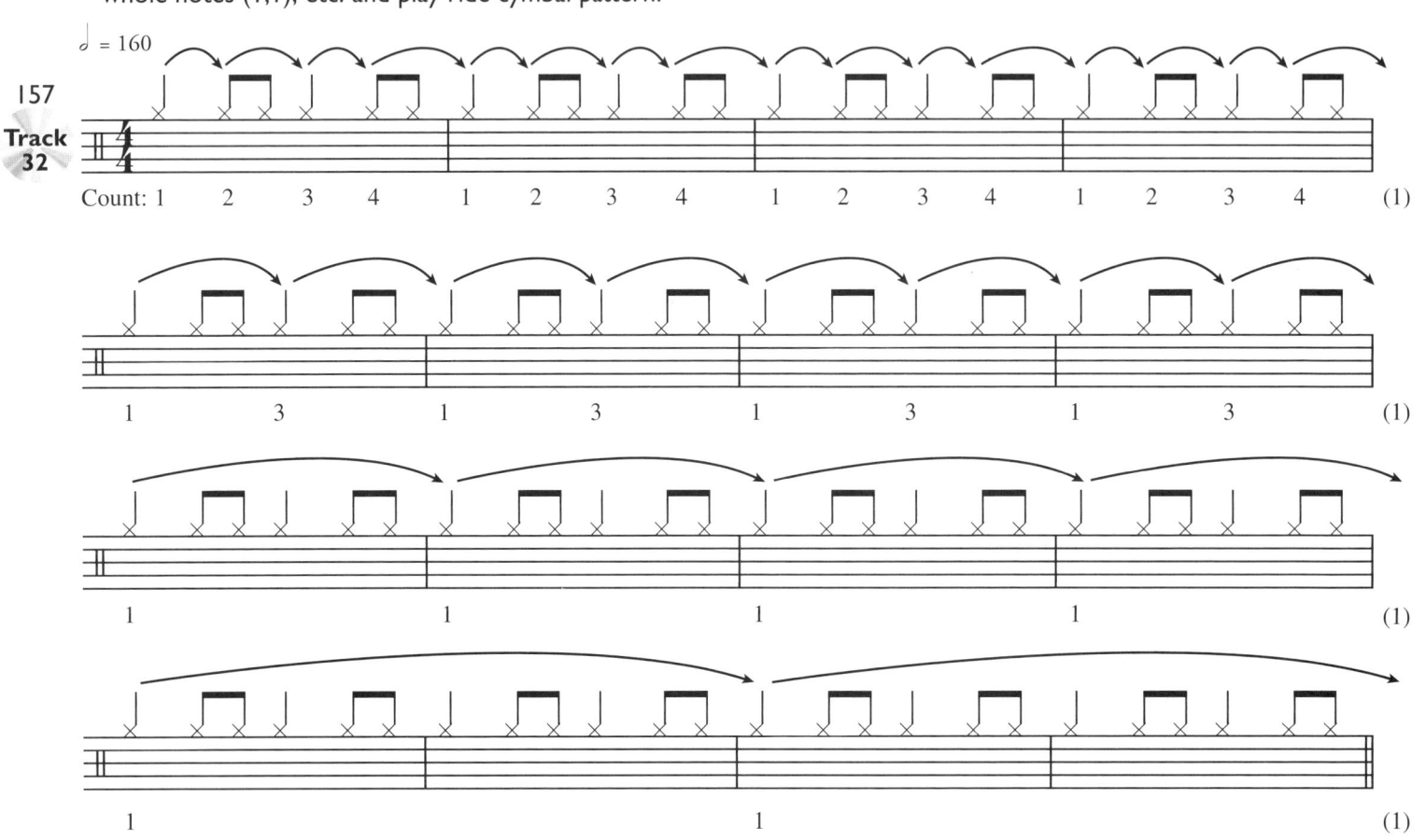

157 Track 32

When playing slow tempos, the opposite occurs. Rather than thinking about whole beats (or groups of multiple beats), try to think about the subdivisions within each beat. When a tempo is very slow, think about the subdivisions and your body will feel a faster pulse, allowing you to stay in time.

Thinking of only the quarter notes or half notes in a slow tempo can have a feeling of unsteadiness, and chances are you will either speed up or, more likely, slow down. Subdividing will allow you to stay in time and maintain the forward momentum.

Try This

Here is a fun and challenging exercise that will show you the importance of mastering both slow and fast tempos. Play any rhythm you like at the slowest metronome marking. Close your eyes, listen to the metronome and play the exact same thing for at least 10 minutes. Now play that same rhythm at various faster metronome markings and notice how much more relaxed your beat is.

158a Track 33.1 — **Counting in Triplets**

158b Track 33.2 — **Counting in Sixteenths**

54 The Total Jazz Drummer

Chapter 7: Coordination

Four-Way Coordination

Now that we've discussed tempos, let's get into further developing coordination between your four limbs. Following is a great exercise that drummer Michael Carvin teaches to strengthen your ability to keep good time while developing your four-way coordination ability.

1. Play eighth notes on all your limbs (hi-hat, snare drum, bass drum and ride cymbal) simultaneously at the slowest metronome marking for 5–10 minutes.

a. Play this exercise as quietly and as evenly as possible.

b. Pay close attention to the sound of all your limbs, making sure each limb is equal in volume to the others. For instance, your bass drum should not be louder than your hi-hat, your ride cymbal should not be louder than your snare drum, and so on.

See below for the notated pattern.

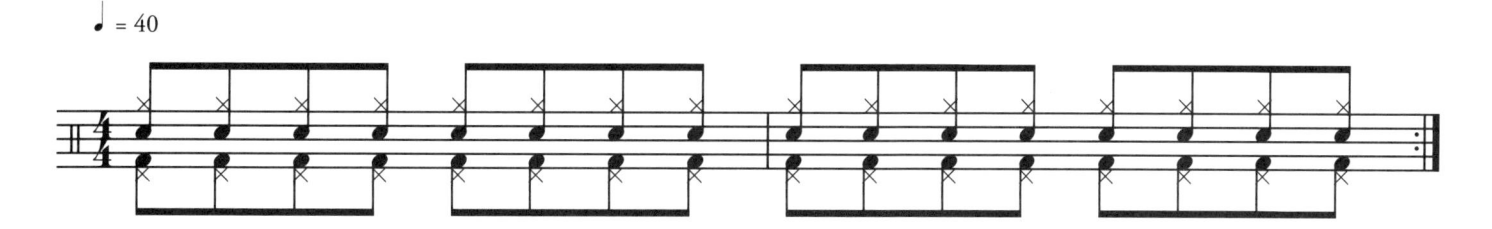

2. After you are comfortable with this, try accenting one limb at a time, while the others stay at a quiet, even volume.

a. Play two bars of all limbs at a quiet volume, then two bars accenting one limb. Then repeat the four bar phrase switching the accent to a different limb.

Track 34 — 159 **Example of Limb Accents**

Coordination Exercises

The coordination exercises that follow (pages 56–69) are a great way to start your practice sessions. They allow you to focus and have better control of your limbs—drumming is about mind over body. Although not written in the exercises, you should play your hi-hat on beats 2 and 4. After you've gone through all the exercises, go back and play the written bass drum part on your hi-hat.

Coordination Exercises

56 The Total Jazz Drummer

The Total Jazz Drummer 57

58 The Total Jazz Drummer

The Total Jazz Drummer 59

60 The Total Jazz Drummer

The Total Jazz Drummer

62 The Total Jazz Drummer

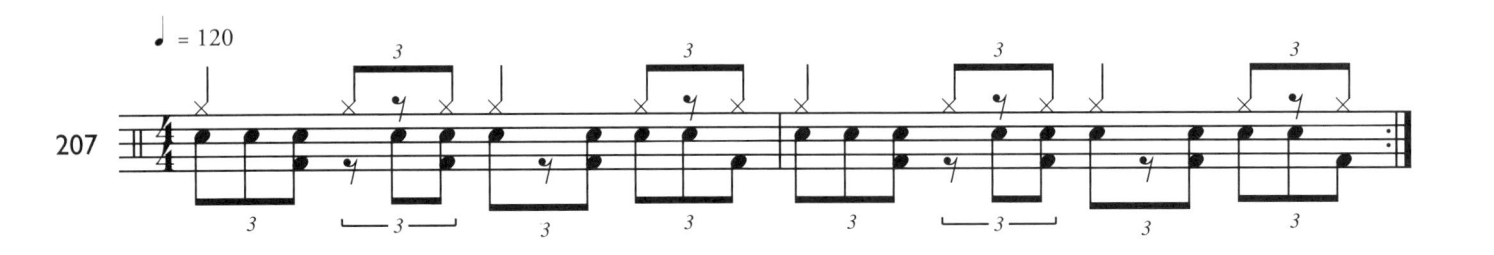

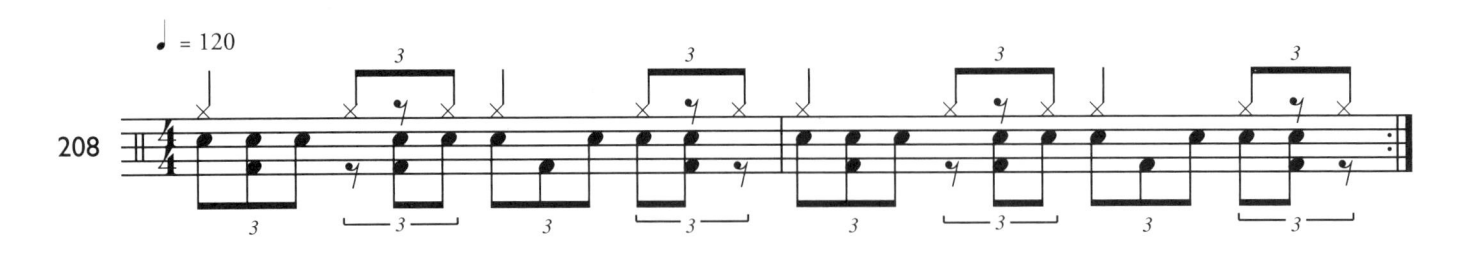

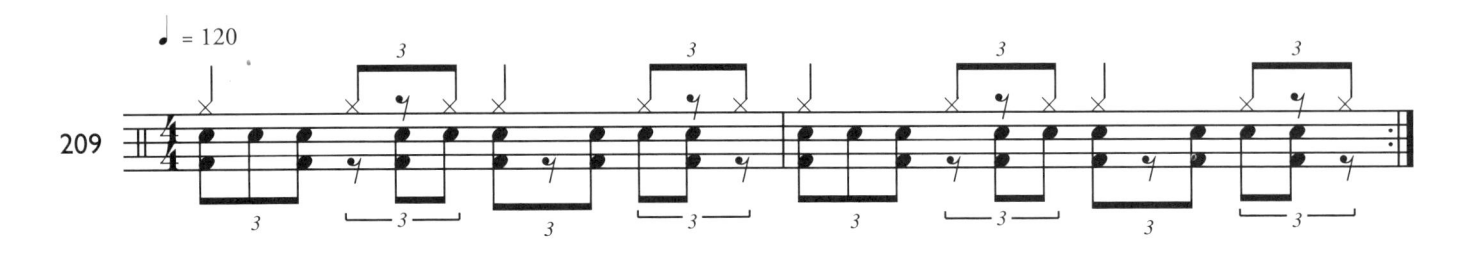

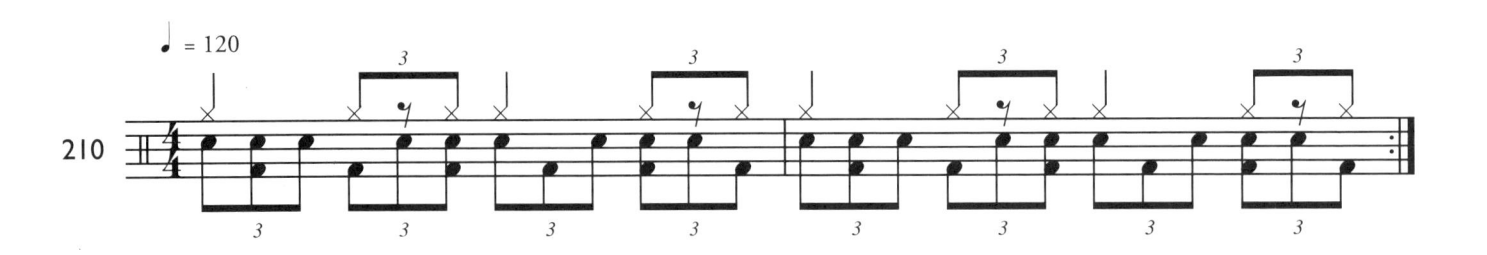

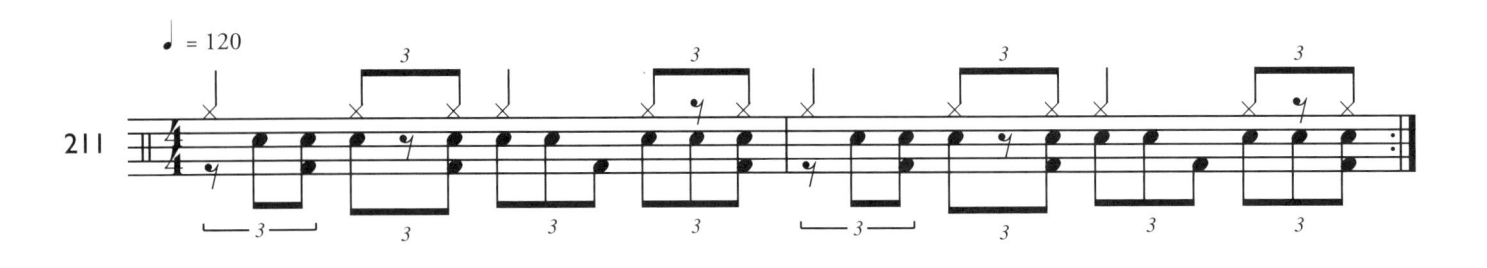

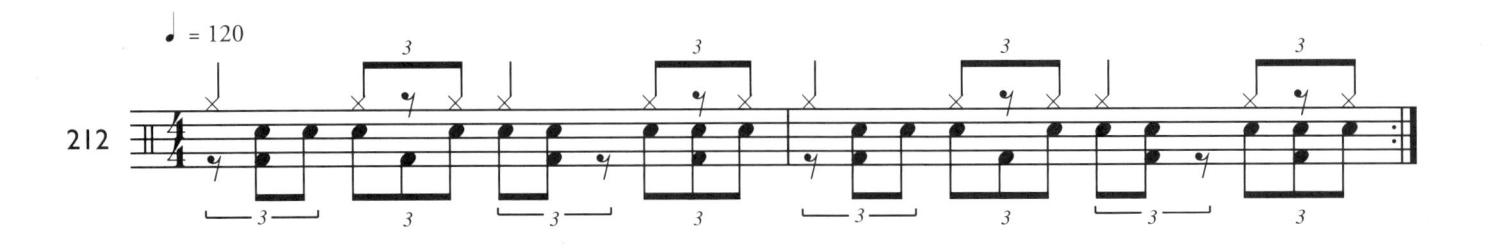

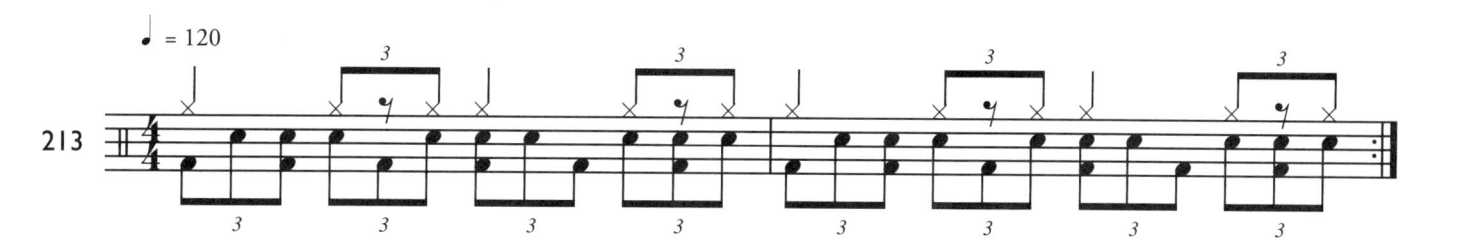

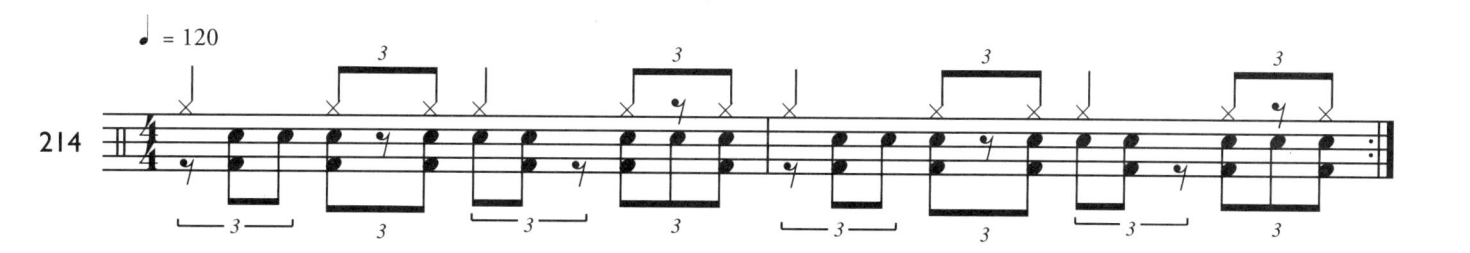

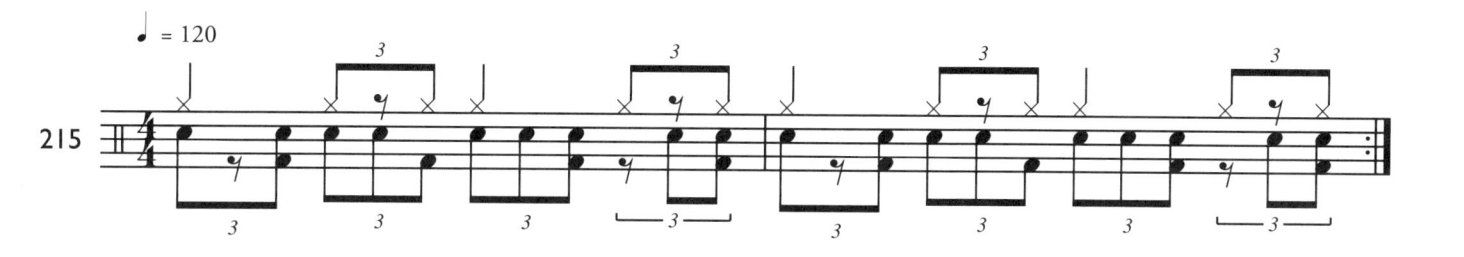

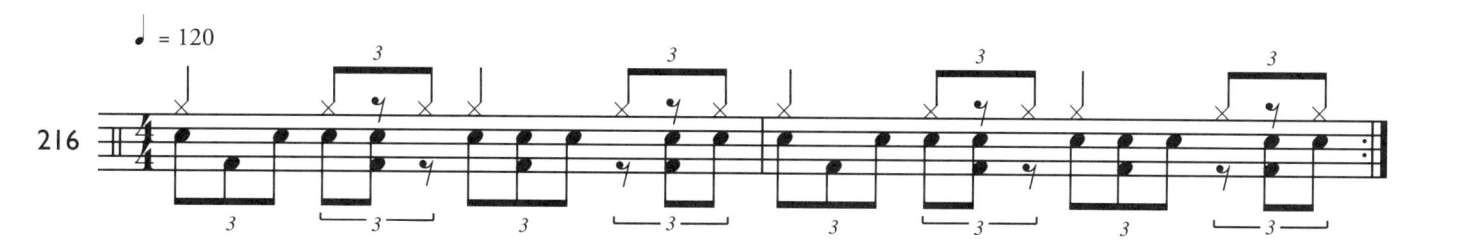

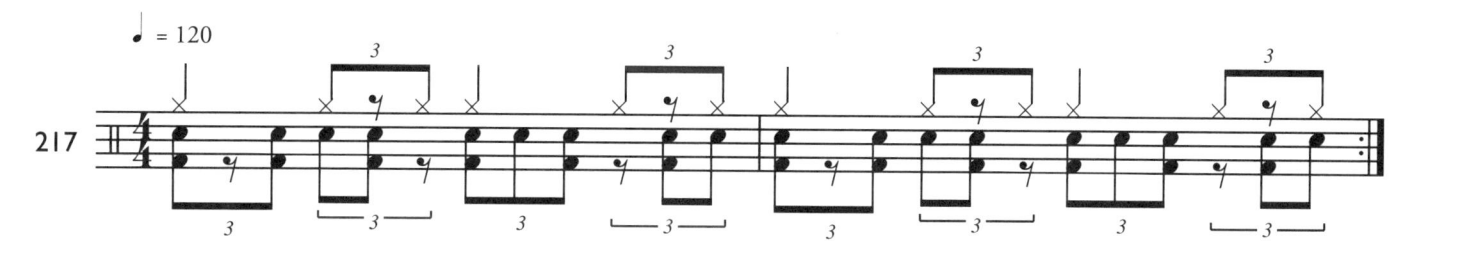

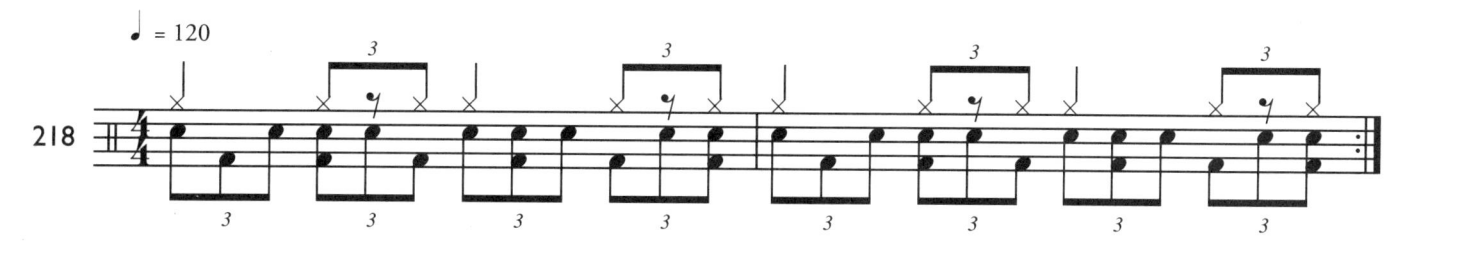

The Total Jazz Drummer

64 The Total Jazz Drummer

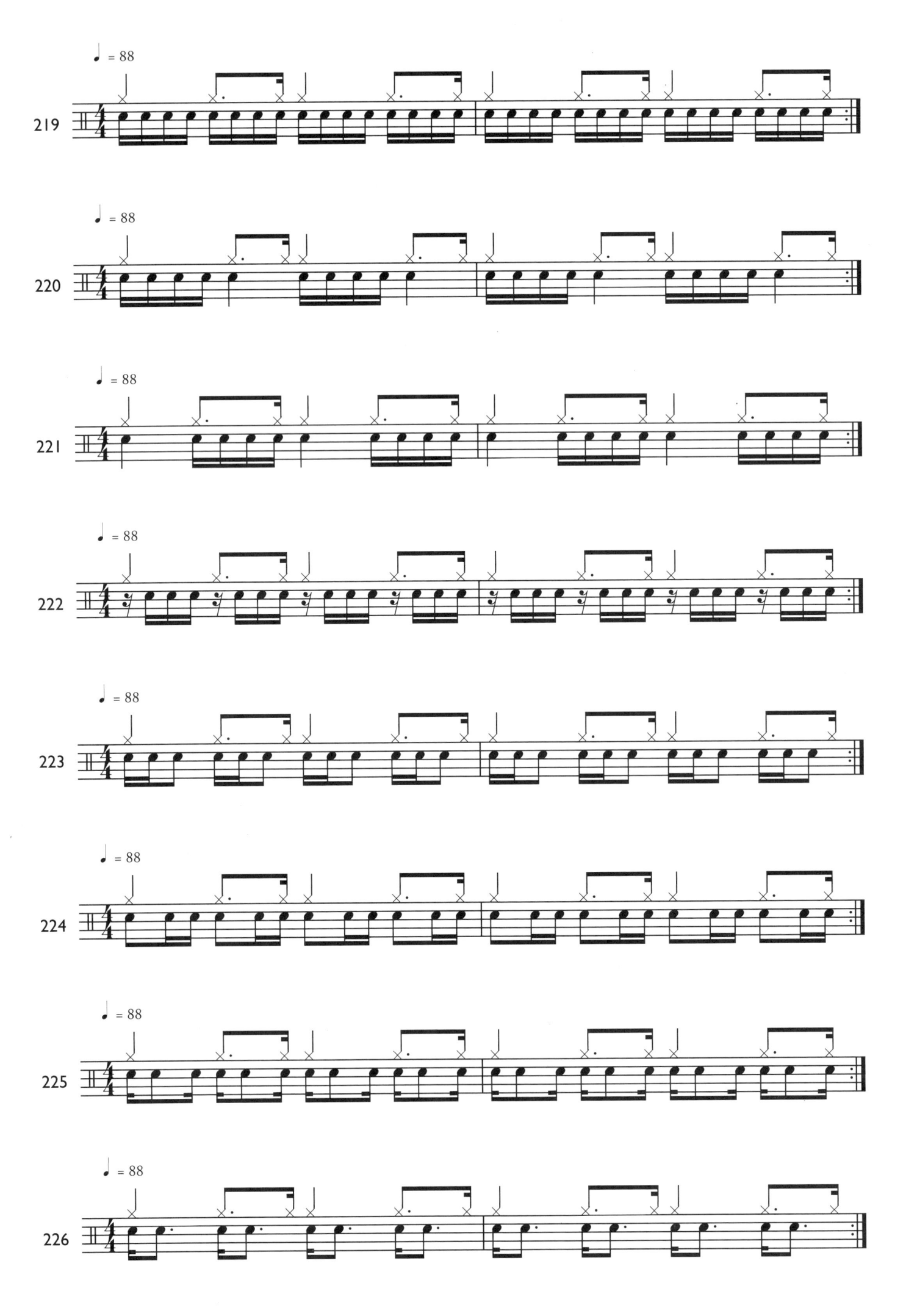

The Total Jazz Drummer 65

66 The Total Jazz Drummer

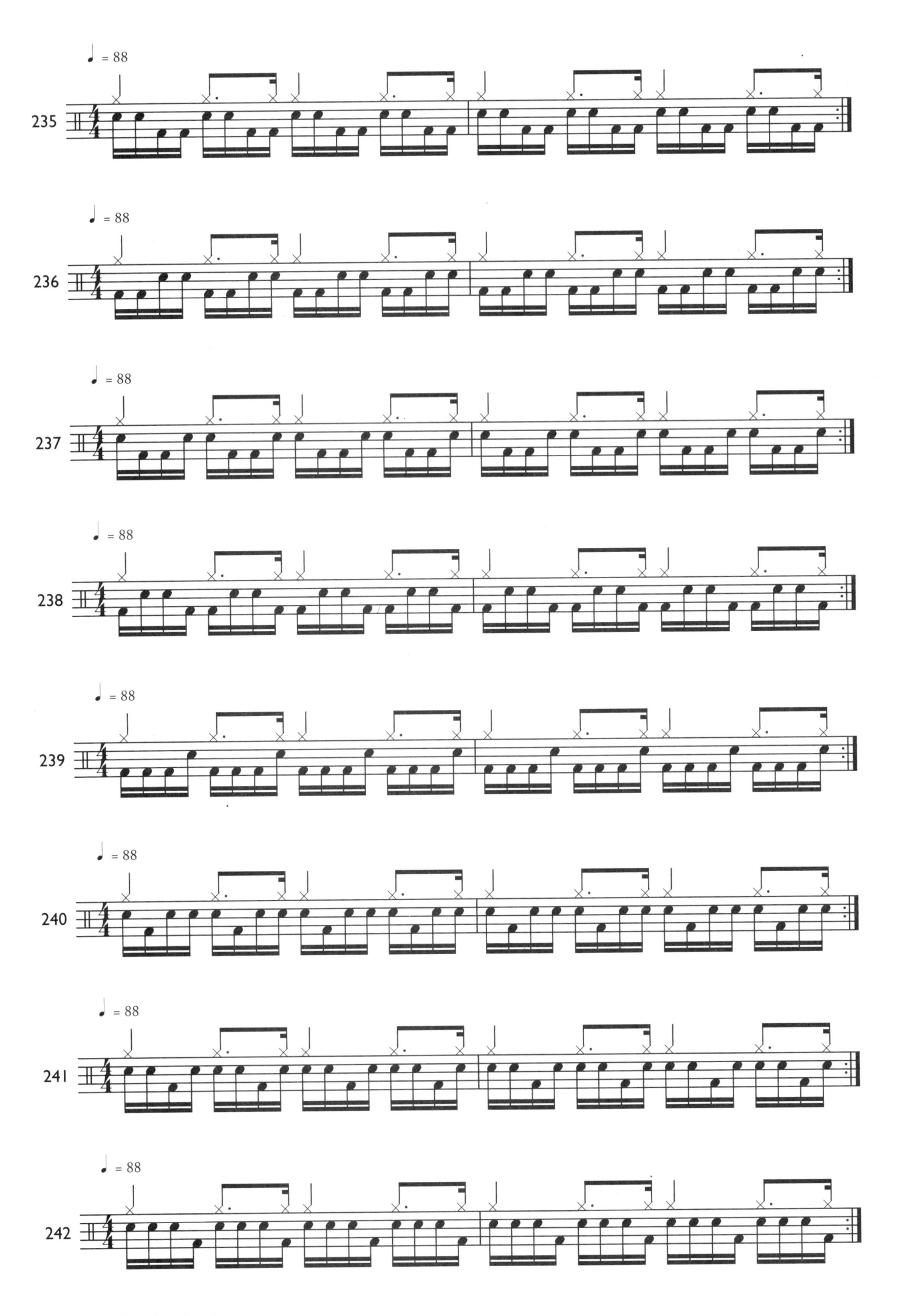

The Total Jazz Drummer

68 The Total Jazz Drummer

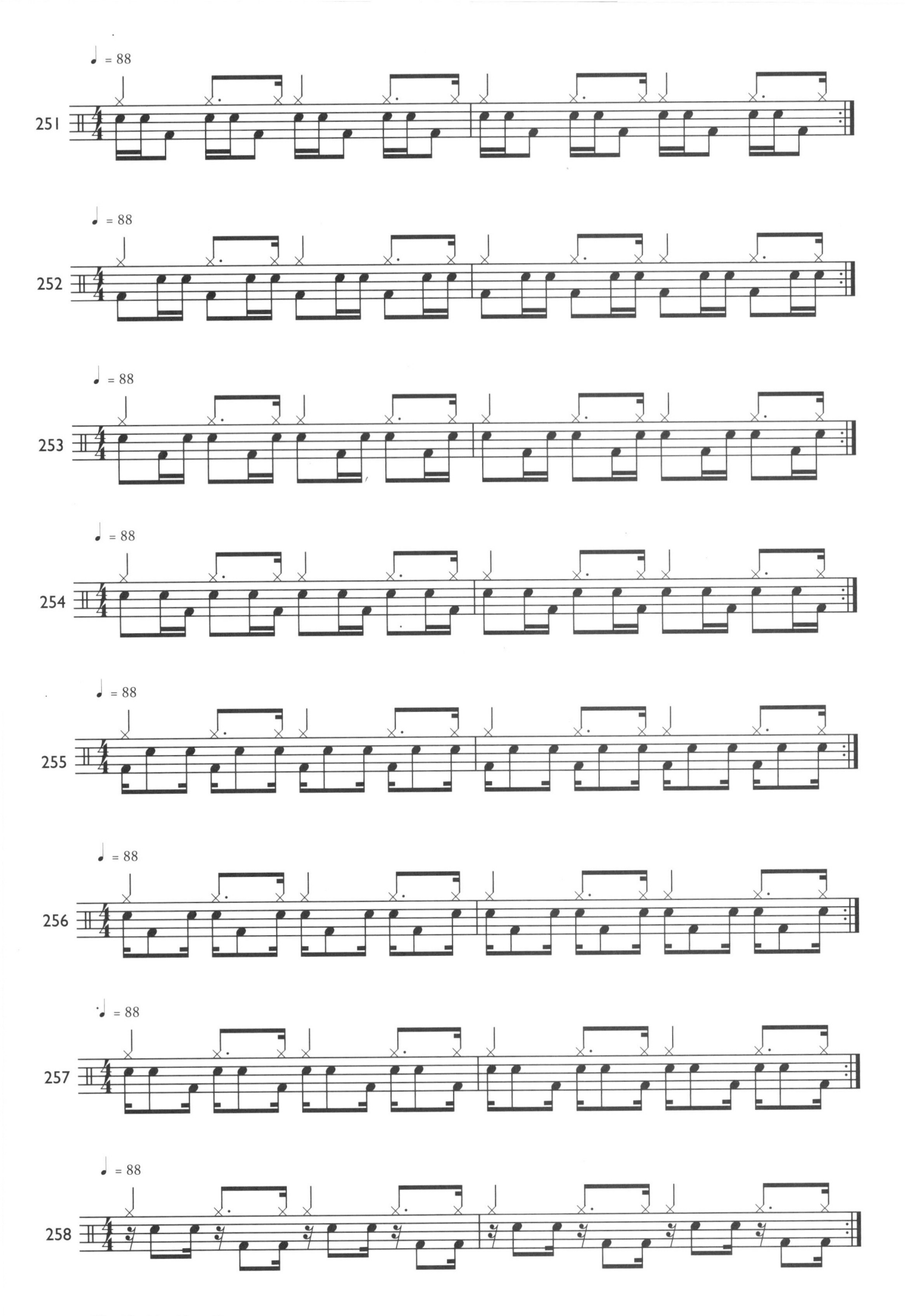

The Total Jazz Drummer

Chapter 8: Fills and Soloing

Just as in other genres of music, knowing how to use *fills* to end a musical phrase or lead into a new section is another key component to being a jazz drummer. Not only are you expected to be an excellent timekeeper who can play a variety of rhythms, but you must also be able to shine as a creative, virtuoso soloist. The four main things to remember in order to play fills and to solo are:

1. Keep a consistent tempo
2. Use your rudiments
3. Utilize all your limbs, not just your hands
4. Be creative

Fill Ideas

For now, let's start off with some fill ideas to get you used to filling in one or two measures at the end of a 4-bar phrase.

Practice variations:
1. During the *bars of time* (the first 2 or 3 measures, before the fill starts), play straight time as written, with the hi-hat on beats 2 and 4.
2. During the bars of time, play the various basic independence exercises we went over in pages 26–27.
3. During the bars of time, play the various coordination exercises we went over in pages 56–69.

One-Bar Fills

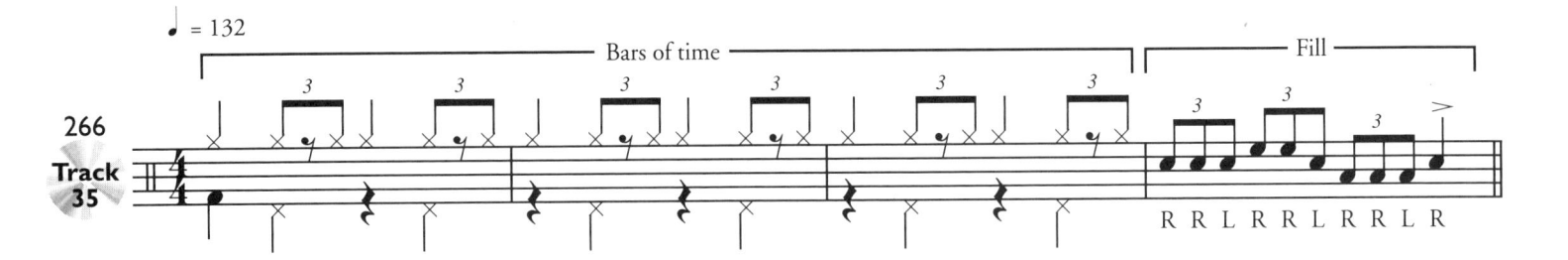

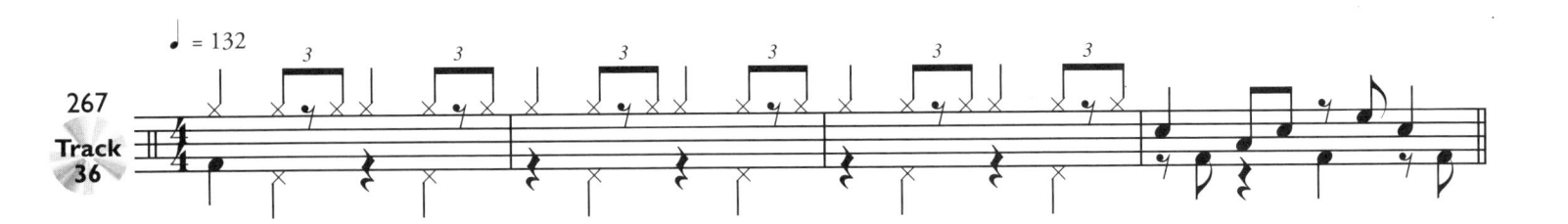

The Total Jazz Drummer   71

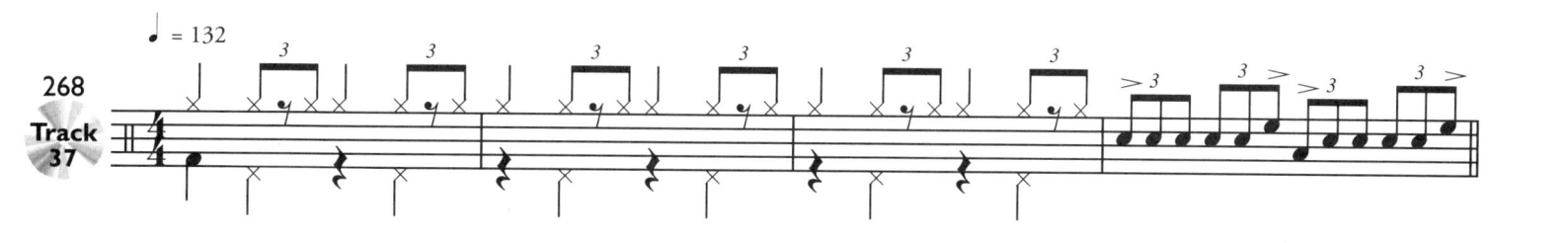

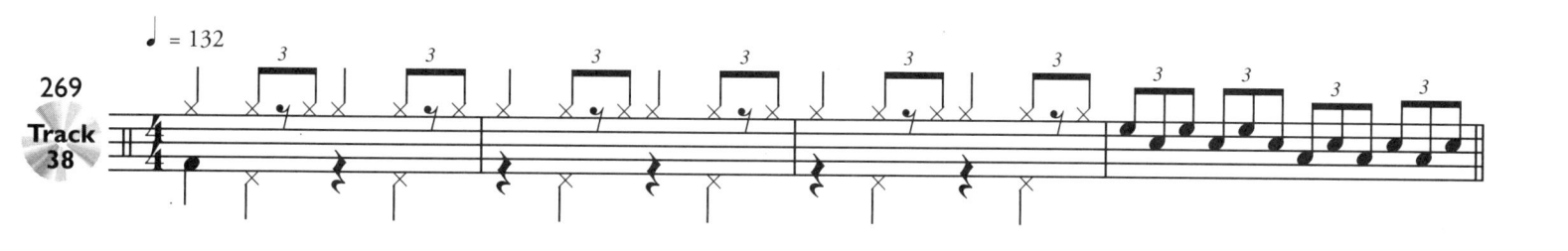

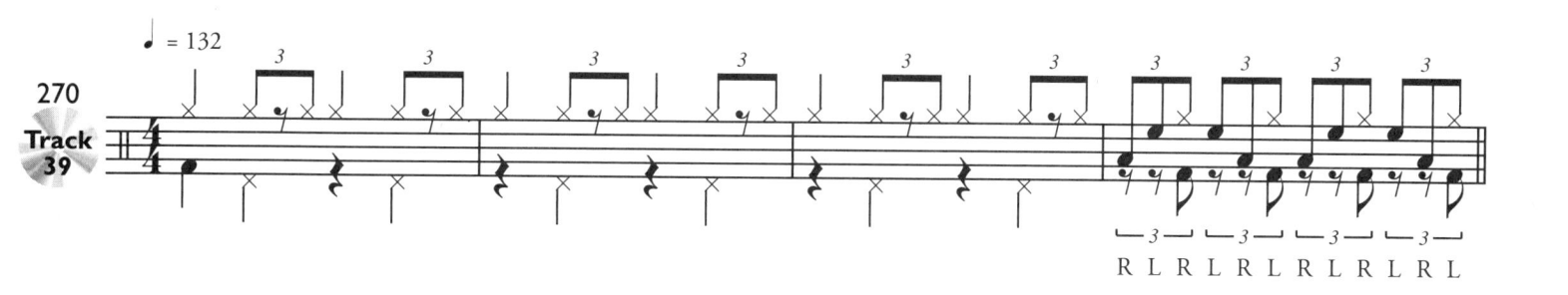

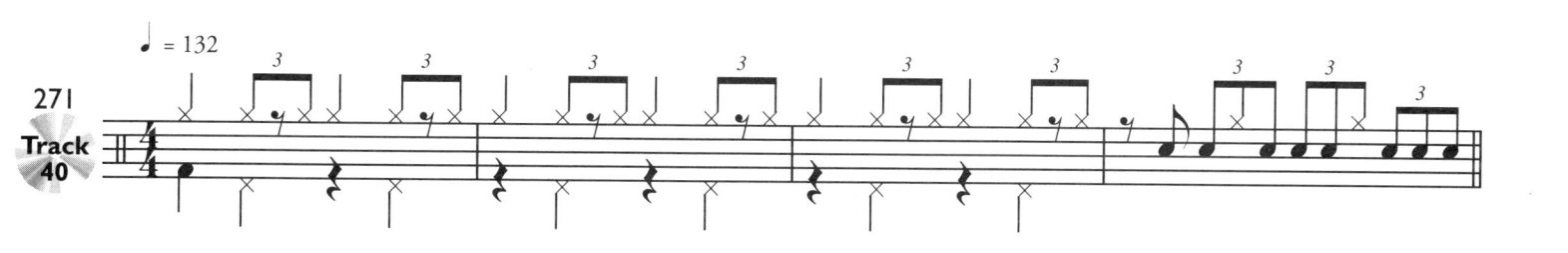

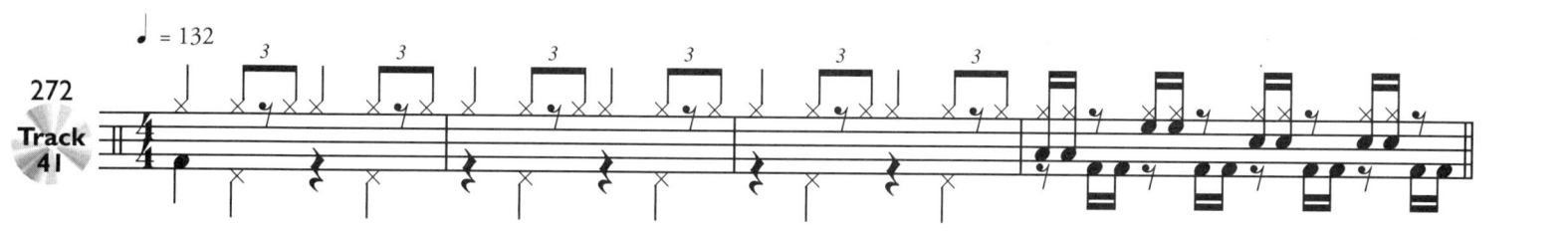

Two-Bar Fills

This crescendo marking tells you to start quietly and gradually get louder.

72   The Total Jazz Drummer

In the Style of Max Roach

Max Roach (b. 1924) was one of the first drummers to play in the bebop style in the 1940s. He performed in bands led by Dizzy Gillespie, Charlie Parker, Thelonious Monk, Coleman Hawkins, Bud Powell and Miles Davis. Ever since the revolutionary 1940s, Roach has stayed at the vanguard of jazz for over 50 years. In 1954, he formed a quintet featuring trumpeter Clifford Brown that was a prime example of the hard bop style. In the 1960s, Roach made a number of albums commenting on racial and political justice. He also recorded the famed trio recording "Money Jungle" with Duke Ellington and Charles Mingus in 1962. In 1970, Roach founded the multi-ethnic percussion group, M'Boom. Max Roach is a jazz drumming pioneer because of his consistently swinging ride cymbal, his many innovative periods and his incredibly melodic drum solos. He is a living legend.

The following are four-bar solos or *breaks* in the style of Max Roach. Play four bars of time and then one of the exercises. Continue with all exercises in this manner.

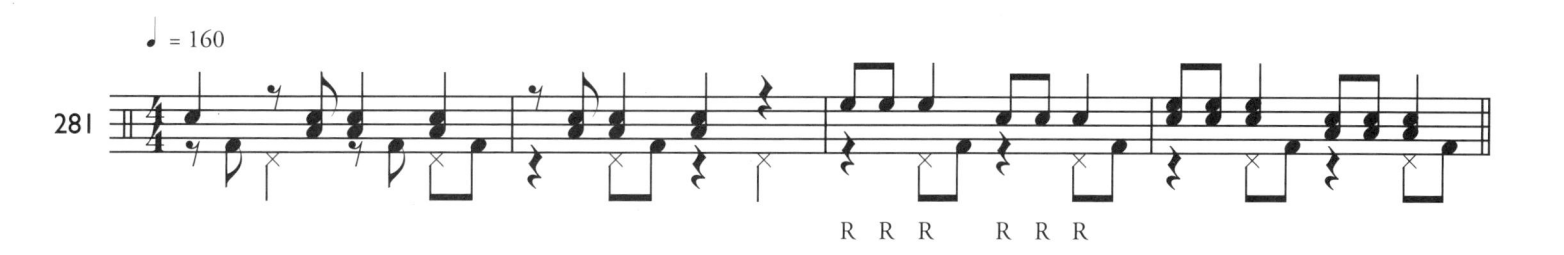

74 The Total Jazz Drummer

In the Style of "Philly" Joe Jones

"Philly" Joe Jones (1923–1985) was a tremendously influential drummer who swung harder than most. He played with the likes of Tadd Dameron and many others before becoming part of the legendary Miles Davis quintet of the 1950s. There are some great Prestige recordings with this group showcasing "Philly" Joe's amazing musicality on the drums. Starting in 1958, Jones recorded many albums as a leader. He eventually moved to England to teach in 1968. Jones returned to the U.S. in the 1970s and in 1980 founded the group Dameronia, celebrating the music of Tadd Dameron. Jones had great precision and energy in his playing. His electrifying solos extended the jazz vocabulary by taking the bass drum out of its traditional role of just providing support and using it to great extent as another drum during his solos.

The following are 4-bar solos or breaks in the style of "Philly" Joe Jones. Play four bars of time and then one of the exercises. Continue with all exercises in this manner. Note that when cross sticking is indicated in the music, you are to use a variation of this technique. You place one stick on the snare and hit it with the other stick (see photo to the right).

A cross sticking variation.

The Total Jazz Drummer

Practice the example below using all right-hand sticking, then all left-hand sticking.

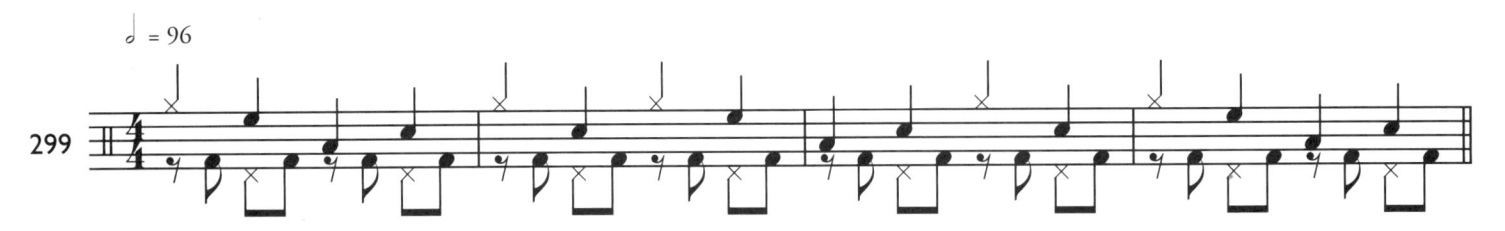

For the next two examples, use the cross sticking variation discussed on page 75.

76 The Total Jazz Drummer

In the Style of Elvin Jones

Elvin Jones (1927–2004) was a one-of-a-kind jazz drummer. He came from a musical family that included brothers Hank (a pianist) and Thad (a trumpet player). After a time in the Army from 1946–1949, Jones returned to Detroit where he was hired by trumpeter Blue Mitchell to back visiting musicians like Charlie Parker and Sonny Stitt. In 1955, Jones moved to New York City where he spent time working with Charles Mingus, Sonny Rollins and John Coltrane. In 1960, Jones joined Coltrane full-time in forming the great John Coltrane Quartet. This quartet made some of the most important music in the history of jazz. What sets Jones apart from other drummers is his rhythmic flow, often compared to West African percussion ensembles. Jones's sense of timing, polyrhythms and dynamics make him one of most influential drummers in the history of jazz.

The following exercises will give you the elements needed to play in the style of Elvin Jones. Try them around the drumset.

302 ♩ = 126
R L L R R L R L L R R L

303 ♩ = 126
R L L R L R L R L R L L

304 ♩ = 126
R L L R L R L L R R L L

305 ♩ = 126
R L R L R L R L R L R L L

306 ♩ = 126
R L R R L L R L R L L

307 ♩ = 126
1. R L R L L R L R L L R L L
2. R L R L R L R L L L R L L
3. R L R L L R L R R L R L

The Total Jazz Drummer   77

Try the following exercises around the drumset. Then, go back and play the hi-hat in place of the bass drum.

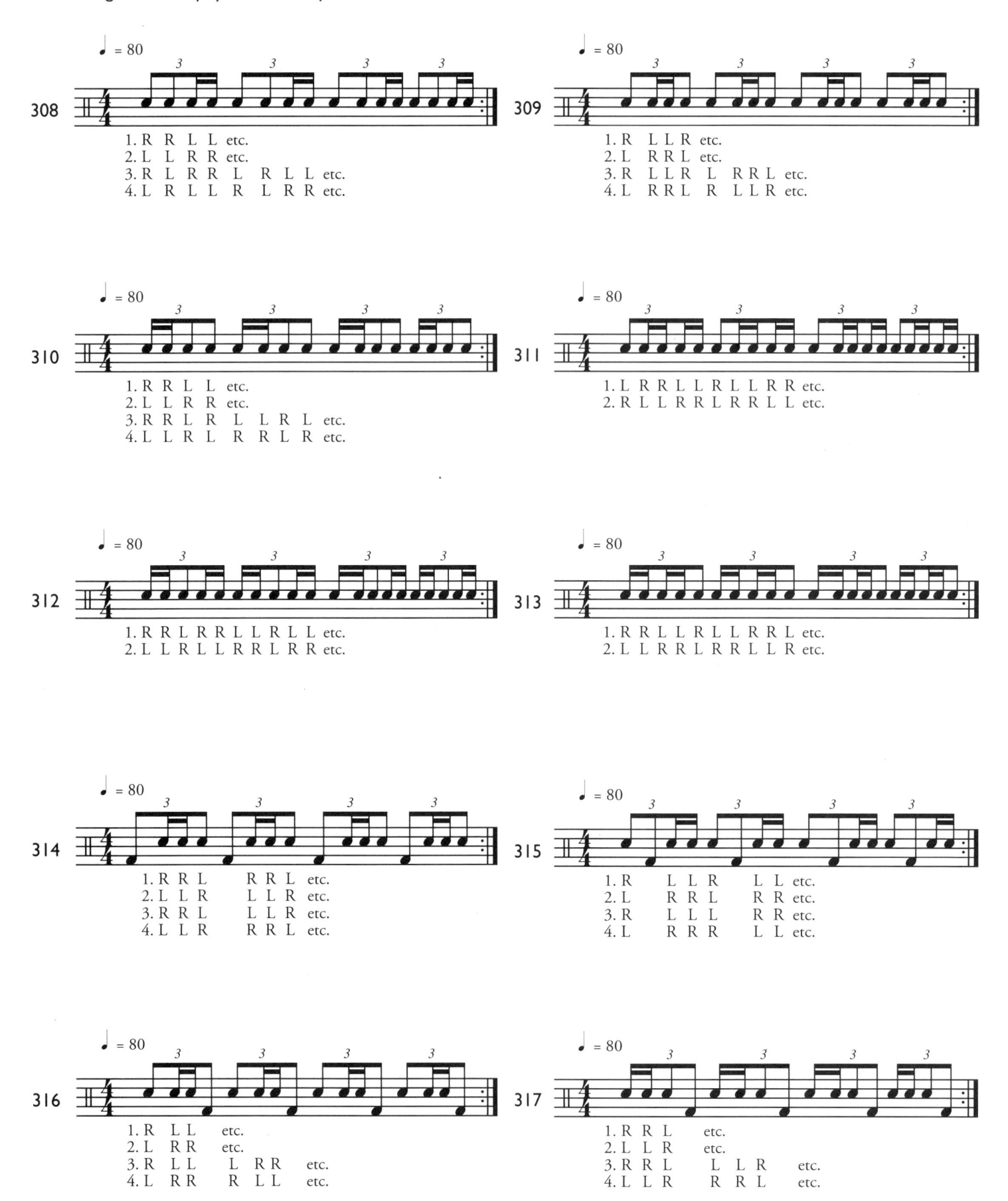

308 ♩ = 80
1. R R L L etc.
2. L L R R etc.
3. R L R R L R L L etc.
4. L R L L R L R R etc.

309 ♩ = 80
1. R L L R etc.
2. L R R L etc.
3. R L L R L R R L etc.
4. L R R L R L L R etc.

310 ♩ = 80
1. R R L L etc.
2. L L R R etc.
3. R R L R L L R L etc.
4. L L R L R R L R etc.

311 ♩ = 80
1. L R R L L R L L R R etc.
2. R L L R R L R R L L etc.

312 ♩ = 80
1. R R L R R L L R L L etc.
2. L L R L L R R L R R etc.

313 ♩ = 80
1. R R L L R L L R R L etc.
2. L L R R L R R L L R etc.

314 ♩ = 80
1. R R L   R R L etc.
2. L L R   L L R etc.
3. R R L   L L R etc.
4. L L R   R R L etc.

315 ♩ = 80
1. R   L L R   L L etc.
2. L   R R L   R R etc.
3. R   L L L   R R etc.
4. L   R R R   L L etc.

316 ♩ = 80
1. R L L   etc.
2. L R R   etc.
3. R L L   L R R   etc.
4. L R R   R L L   etc.

317 ♩ = 80
1. R R L   etc.
2. L L R   etc.
3. R R L   L L R   etc.
4. L L R   R R L   etc.

78   The Total Jazz Drummer

318
♩ = 80

1. R R L etc.
2. L L R etc.
3. R R L L L R etc.
4. L L R R R L etc.

319
♩ = 80

1. L R R L R R etc.
2. R L L R L L etc.
3. L R R R L L etc.
4. R L L L R R etc.

320
♩ = 80

1. R R L L etc.
2. L L R R etc.
3. R R L L L L R R etc.
4. L L R R R R L L etc.

321
♩ = 80

1. R R L L etc.
2. L L R R etc.
3. R R L L L L R R etc.
4. L L R R R R L L etc.

322
♩ = 80

1. R R L L etc.
2. L L R R etc.
3. R R R R L L R R etc.
4. L L L L R R L L etc.

323
♩ = 80

1. R R R R etc.
2. L L L L etc.
3. R R L L etc.
4. L L R R etc.

324
♩ = 80

1. R R etc.
2. L L etc.
3. R R L L etc.
4. L L R R etc.

325
♩ = 80

1. R R etc.
2. L L etc.
3. R R L L etc.
4. L L R R etc.

The Total Jazz Drummer

Mix and match examples A–R from beat to beat.

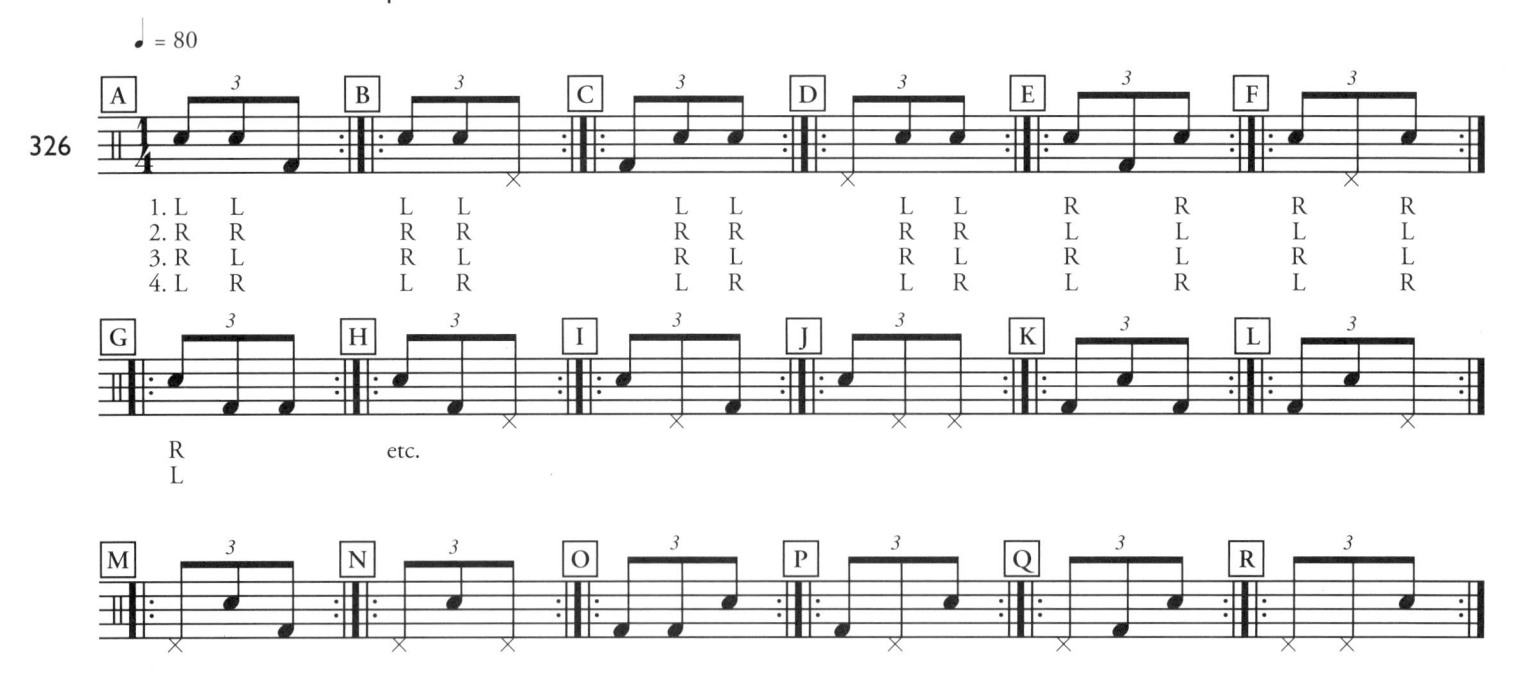

♩ = 80

1. L L L L L L L L R R R R
2. R R R R R R R R L L L L
3. R L R L R L R L R L R L
4. L R L R L R L R L R L R

R
L   etc.

The following are one-bar breaks in the style of Elvin Jones.
Play three bars of time and then one of the exercises.

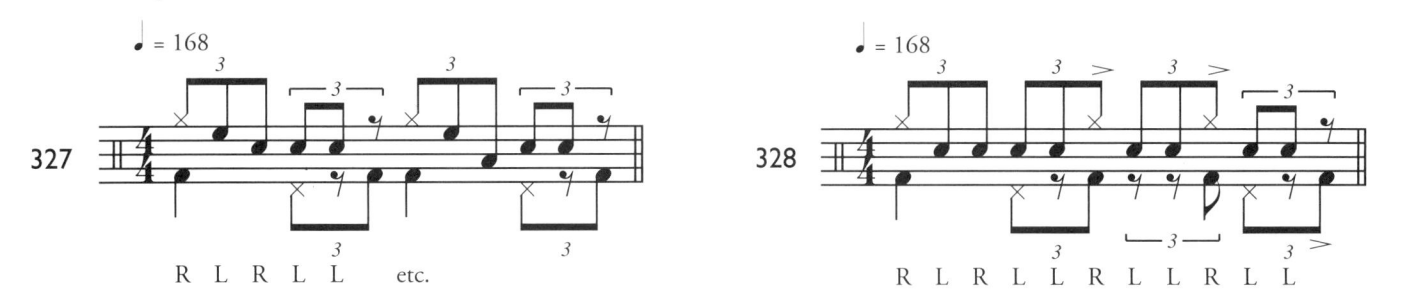

♩ = 168

327: R L R L L   etc.

♩ = 168

328: R L R L L R L L R L L

Play two bars of time before each of the following exercises.

♩ = 168

329: R L R L L   R   etc.

♩ = 168

330: R L L R L R R   etc.
              L

♩ = 168

331: R   R
      L L   L L   L L   etc.

80 The Total Jazz Drummer

In the Style of Tony Williams

Tony Williams (1945–1997) was one of the masters of jazz drumming. At the age of 13, he was already playing professionally with Sam Rivers in Boston. Shortly after being hired by Jackie McLean at age 16, Williams moved to New York City to begin his famed stint with Miles Davis's pivotal 1960s band (the "Second Great Quintet"). In 1969, this virtuoso drummer started his famed Lifetime band, which was a pioneering fusion band until the late '70s. He continued his prolific career leading various bands, recording, touring and teaching, until his sudden death at the age of 51. Williams was known for his great command of polyrhythms and metric modulations *(transitioning between mathematically related tempos and/or time signatures). His ability to play extremely fast tempos was also matched by his tremendous ability to play with his feet as naturally and musically as with his hands. He was a true revolutionary in jazz drumming history.*

The following are two-bar breaks in the style of Tony Williams. Play two bars of time before each of the following exercises.

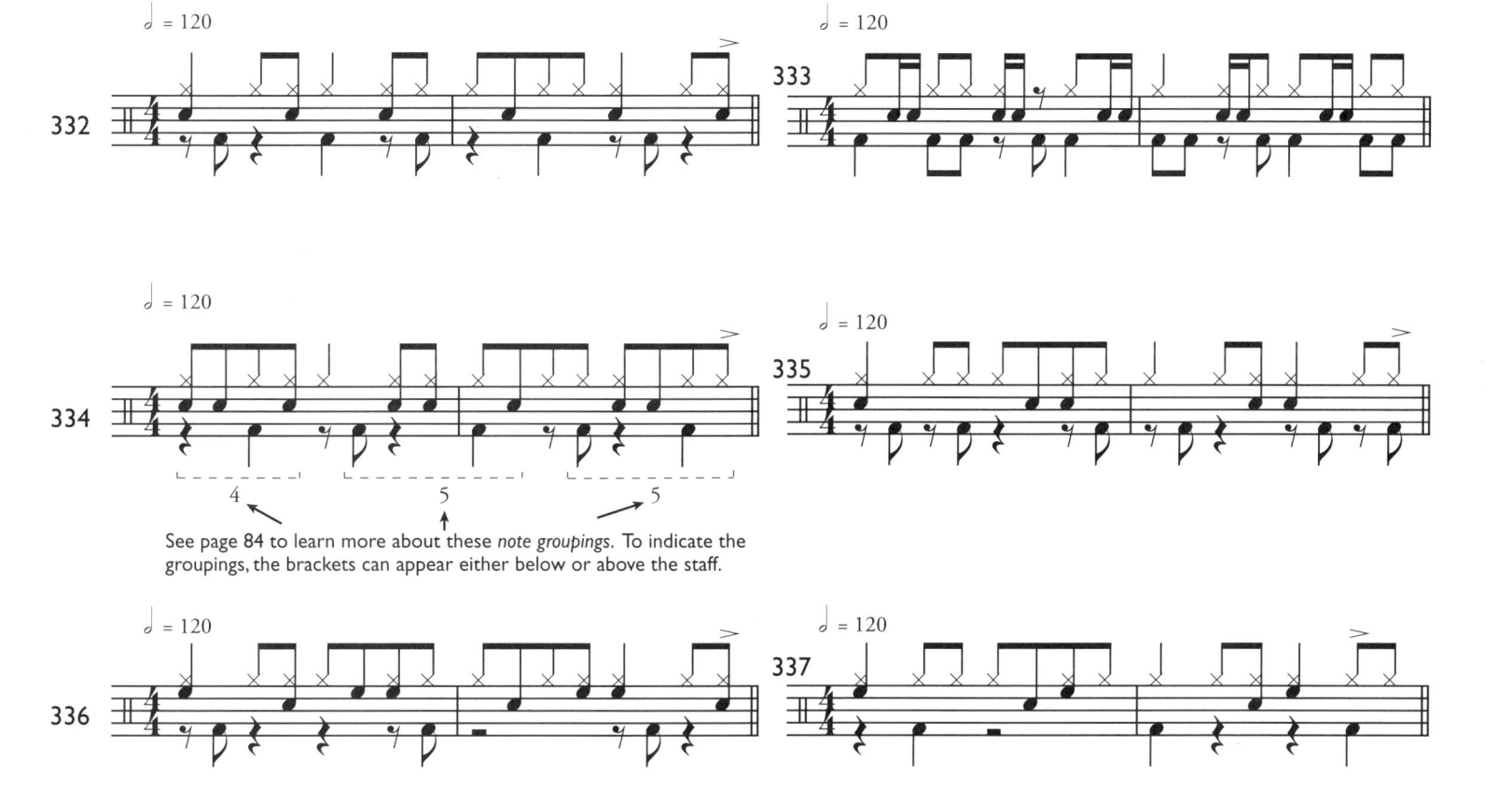

See page **84** to learn more about these *note groupings*. To indicate the groupings, the brackets can appear either below or above the staff.

The Total Jazz Drummer 81

Play four bars of time before each of the following exercises.

A *tie* connects two notes. The sound of the first note should continue for the duration of the next note.

Play two bars of time before each of the following exercises.

PART 3: The Advanced Jazz Drummer

Practicing

Welcome to Part 3. At this point, you have a firm foundation in playing jazz drums, and now you're on your way to becoming a virtuoso soloist. We're going to delve deeper into the rhythmic possibilities of jazz drumming. First, let's add to your practice routine from Parts 1 and 2:

- Continue practicing the fundamentals and various styles, but work on developing your own unique style as well.

- Increase your practice time to a minimum of two hours a day, seven days week. The more you practice, the better chance you'll have of developing your own unique style.

- Play with other musicians. Playing is different than practicing, and the only way to become a good ensemble player is to play with as many people as possible.

- Listen to all types of music. Being a jazz musician means being open-minded and absorbing all types of sound.

- Study with as many teachers as possible. Get different perspectives. Never stop studying, no matter what your age. There is always something to learn.

- Remember, practicing means working on the things that you cannot yet play on the drumset, not jamming on stuff that you can already play.

Chapter 9: Linear Phrasing

Linear phrasing, also known as *linear drumming* or *interdependence*, deals with *note groupings*, and is great for developing fluidity, timing and groove. Linear phrasing has to do with the way in which you phrase or interpret a single line of figures. For example, there are multiple ways to play a 4/4 measure of eighth notes, depending on what drums/cymbals you hit and where you place accents. So, if we look first at the different ways of playing this measure just using accents, we find that note groupings produce numerous phrasing possibilities:

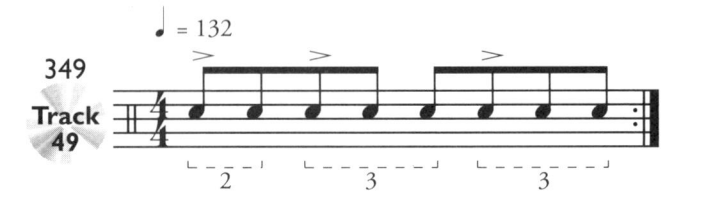

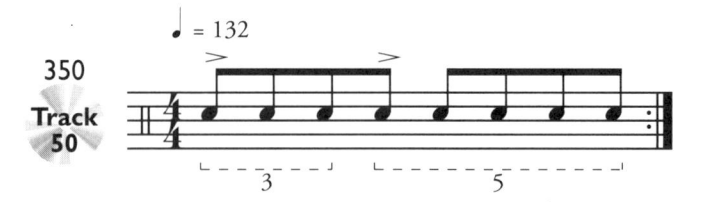

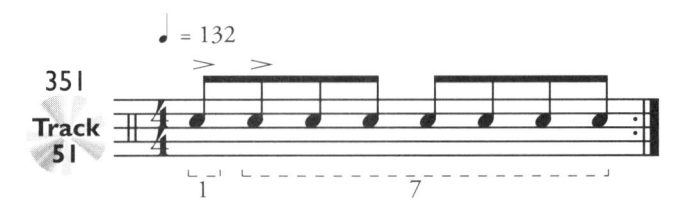

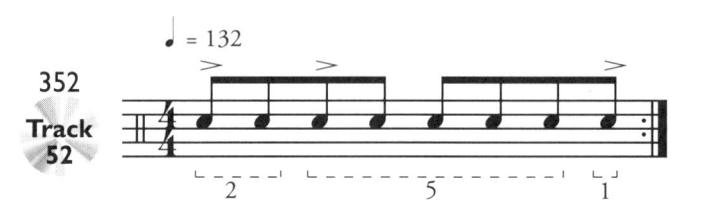

Now, let's play these examples on the drumset.

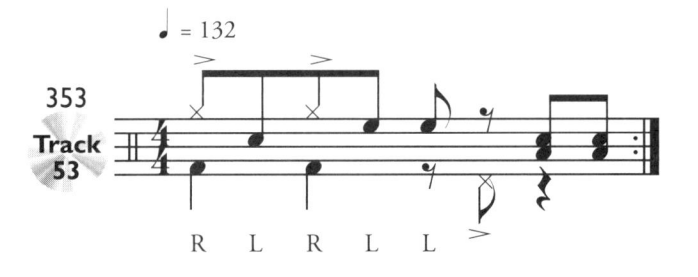

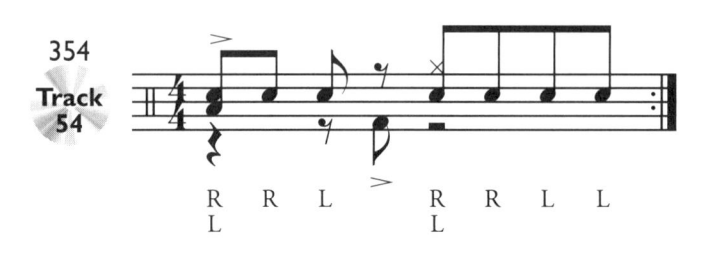

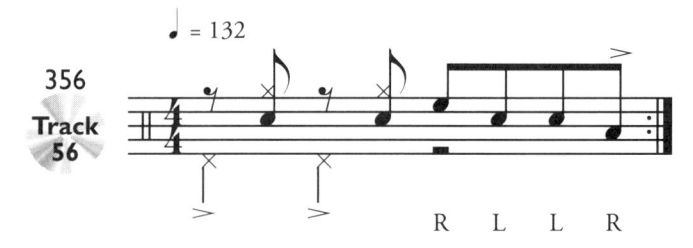

84   The Total Jazz Drummer

This idea of linear phrasing opens a big door in the world of rhythm and allows you to get as creative as you want. Tony Williams was a master of linear phrasing, and his playing and soloing are great examples of this. Many drummers have since come along and approached drumming with this concept.

Steps to developing your linear drumming skills

1. With your hands, practice playing a constant line of eighth notes at a comfortable metronome marking.

2. Without breaking the flow of your line, start mixing up your sticking.

3. Get to the point where you are not thinking about your sticking and are able to mix it up with ease.

4. Start to incorporate accents into your single line, while still mixing up your sticking.

5. Move your right hand to the floor tom and continue with what you were doing. Hear the inherent melodies that are being created.

6. Now, move your hands around the drums.

7. Go back and now incorporate your feet in this process, by alternating and playing simultaneously with your hands.

8. Again, move your hands around the drums while still incorporating your feet.

9. Now, practice this from the beginning using triplets.

Snare Drum Accents

We'll now go through a series of exercises that will enhance your ability to drum in a linear fashion. The following pages present eighth notes, triplets and sixteenth notes grouped in threes, fours, fives and sevens. For now, play your bass drum on all four beats and your hi-hat on beats 2 and 4.

Three-Note Groupings

Below are some different stickings to use with the following exercises, but you should come up with your own as well.

Stickings:

1. RLR LRL
2. LRL RLR
3. RLL
4. LRR
5. LLR
6. RRL
7. RLR RLR
8. LRL LRL
9. RRR LLL
10. LLL RRR

Three-Note Groupings: Eighth Notes

357

Three-Note Groupings: Triplets

Three-Note Groupings: Sixteenth Notes

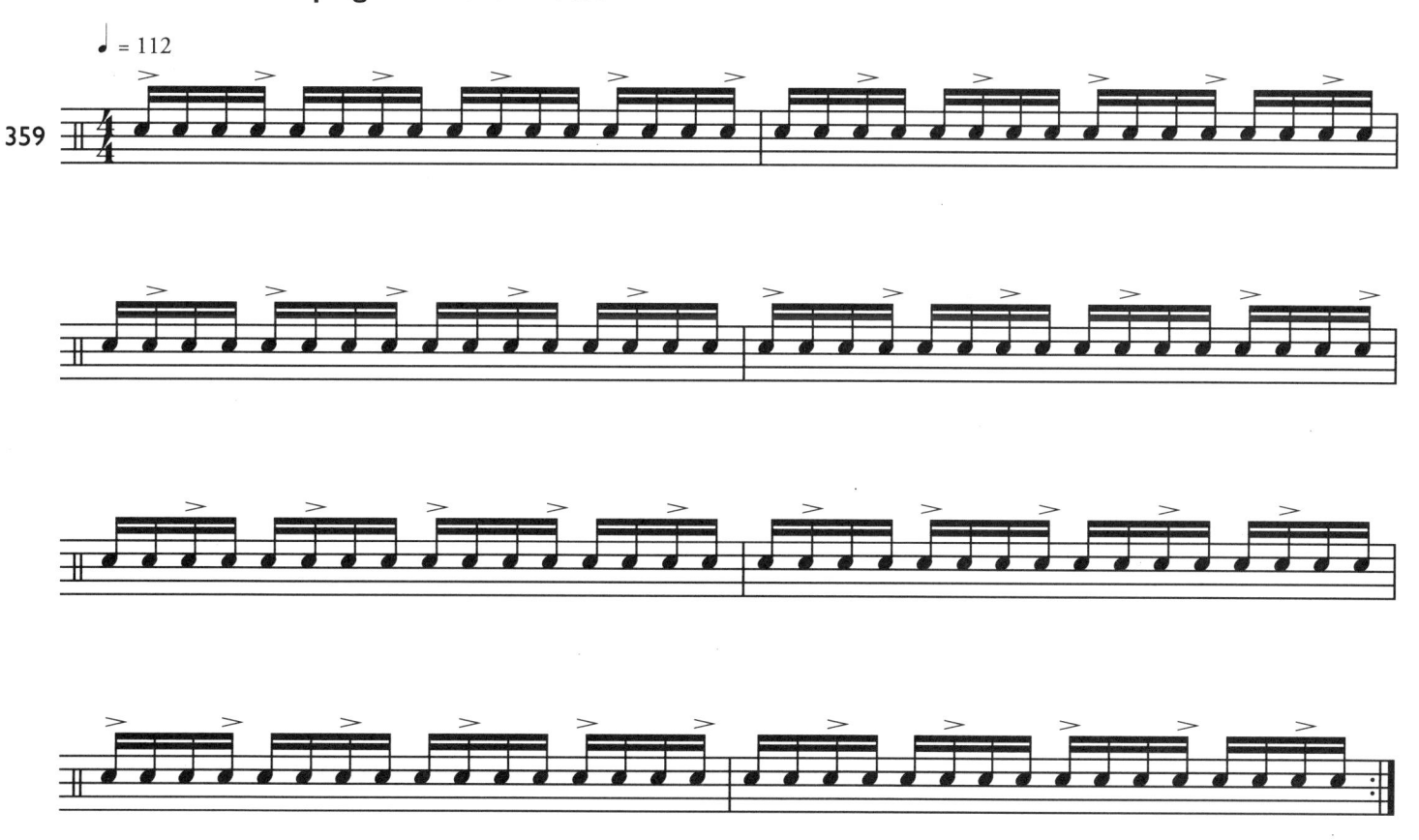

Four-Note Groupings

Stickings:
1. RLRL
2. LRLR
3. RRLL
4. LLRR
5. RLRR LRLL
6. LRLL RLRR
7. RLLR RLLR
8. LRRL LRRL
9. RRLR LLRL
10. LLRL RRLR

Four-Note Groupings: Eighth Notes

♩ = 112

360

Four-Note Groupings: Triplets

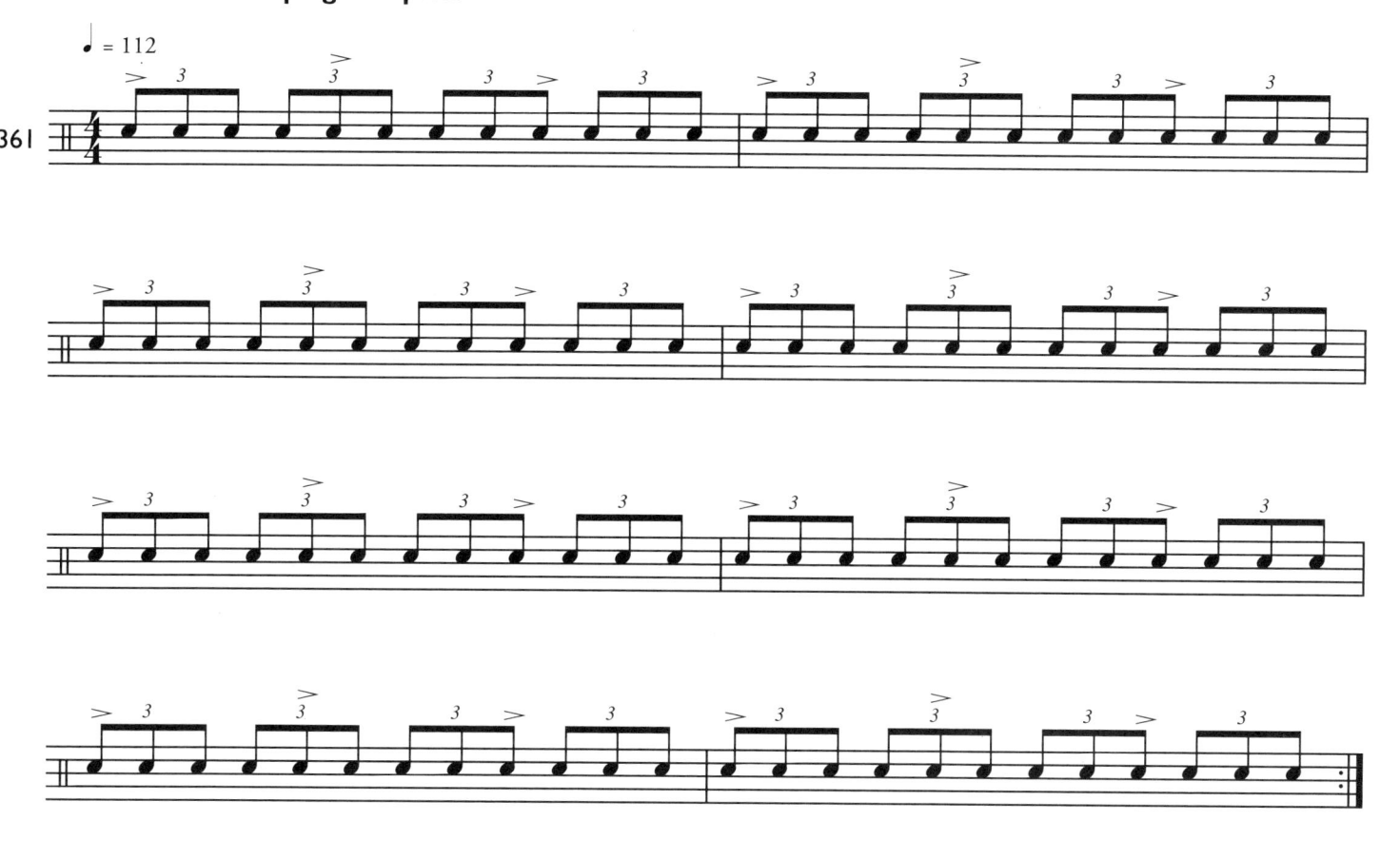

Four-Note Groupings: Sixteenth Notes

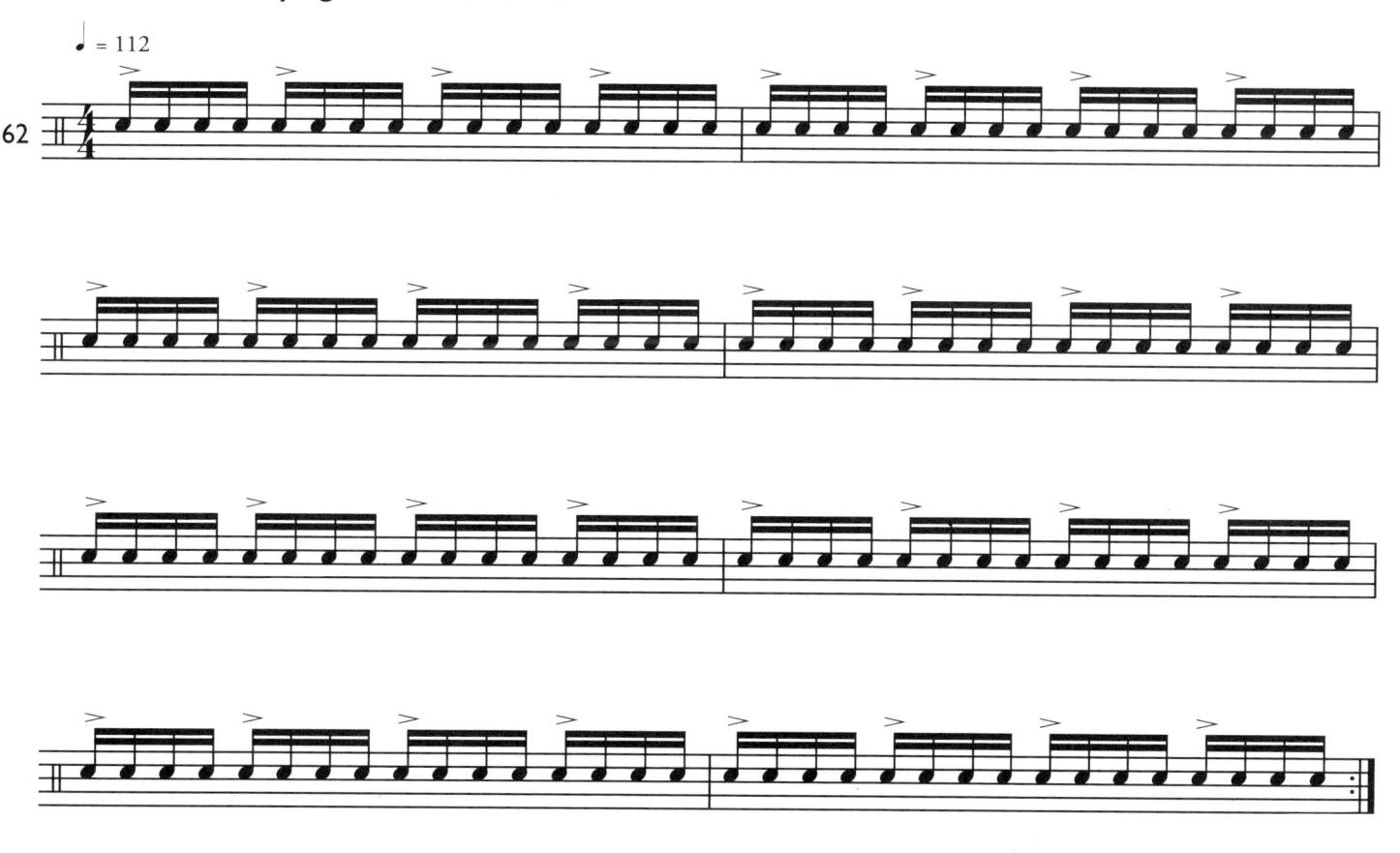

Five-Note Groupings

Stickings:
1. RLRLR LRLRL
2. LRLRL RLRLR
3. RLRLL
4. LRLRR
5. RRLLR LLRRL
6. LLRRL RRLLR
7. RRLLR RLLRR LLRRL LRRLL
8. LLRRL LRRLL RRLLR RLLRR
9. RLLRL
10. LRRLR

Five-Note Groupings: Eighth Notes

Five-Note Groupings: Triplets

Five-Note Groupings: Sixteenth Notes

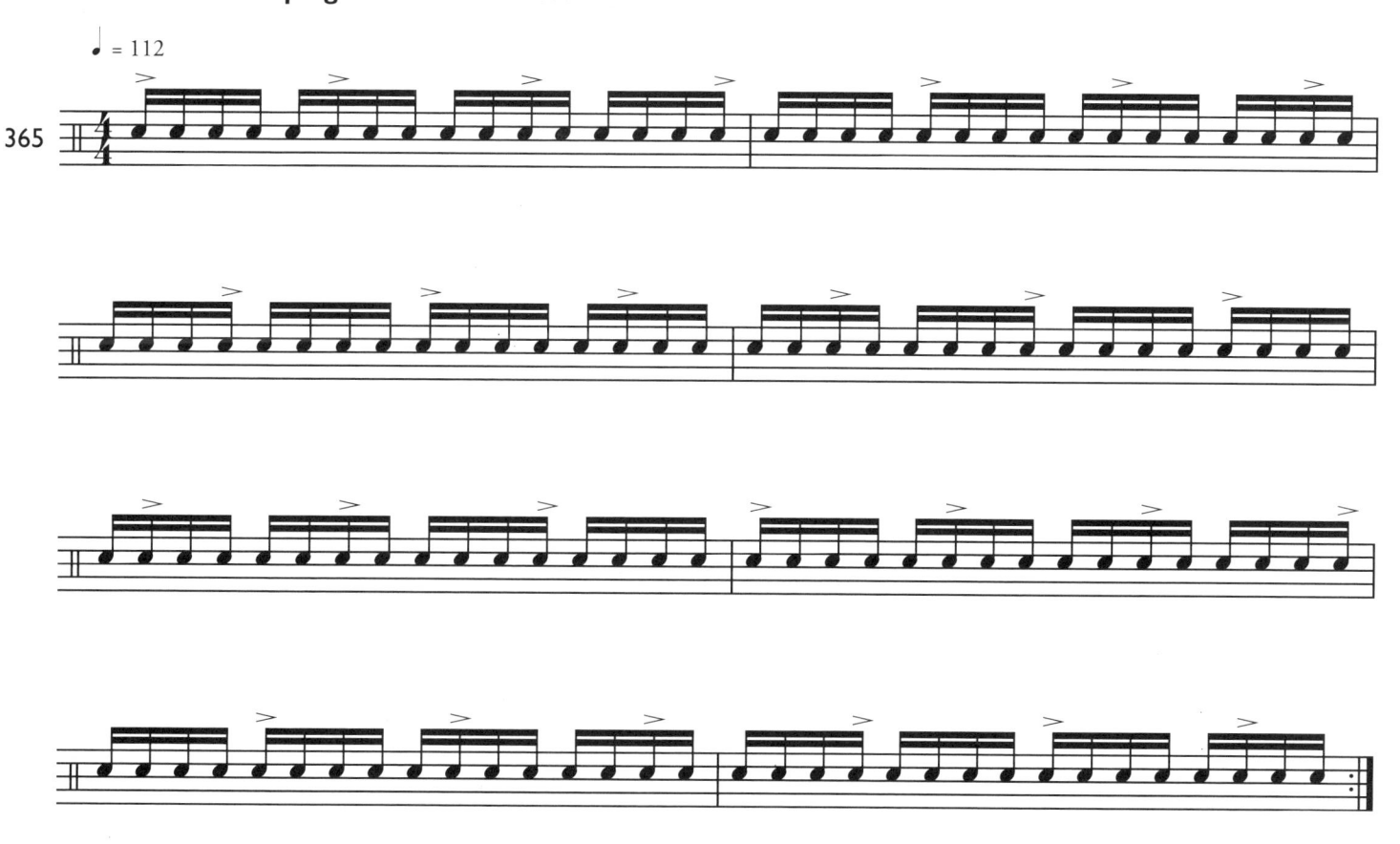

Seven-Note Groupings

Stickings:

1. RLRLRLR LRLRLRL
2. LRLRLRL RLRLRLR
3. RLRLRLL
4. LRLRLRR
5. RRLLRRL
6. LLRRLLR
7. RRLLRRL LRRLLRR LLRRLLR RLLRRLL
8. LLRRLLR RLLRRLL RRLLRRL LRRLLRR
9. RLLRLRL
10. LRRLRLR

Seven-Note Groupings: Eighth Notes

Seven-Note Groupings: Triplets

Seven-Note Groupings: Sixteenth Notes

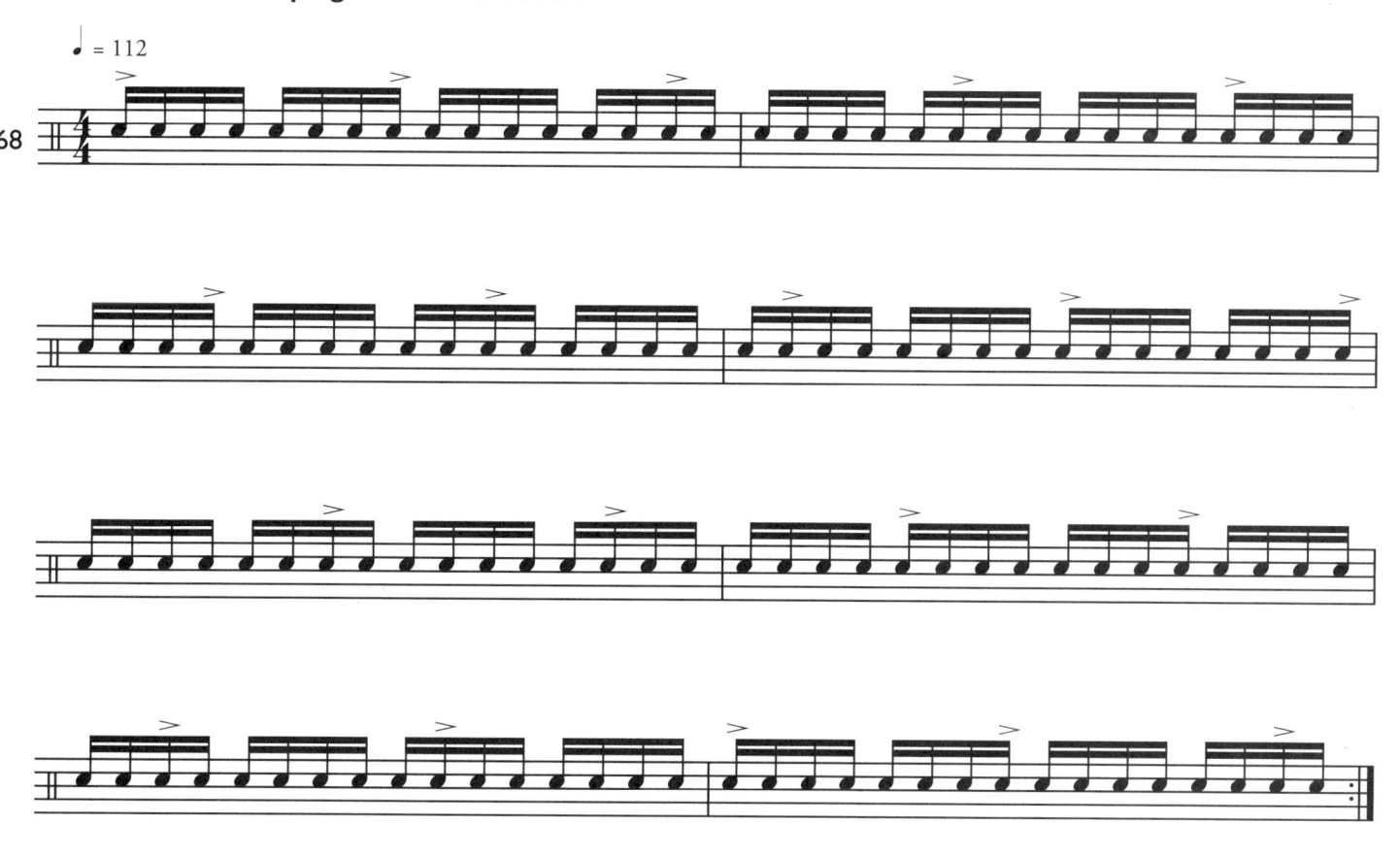

Bass Drum and Cymbal Accents

The following pages have eighth notes, triplets and sixteenth notes grouped in threes, fours, fives and sevens. Play the exercises by placing the accents on your bass drum and cymbals, while the unaccented beats are played on the snare drum. Play your hi-hat on all four beats as well.

Three-Note Groupings

Stickings:

1. RLR LRL
2. LRL RLR
3. RLL
4. LRR
5. LLR
6. RRL
7. RLR RLR
8. LRL LRL
9. RRR LLL
10. LLL RRR

Three-Note Groupings: Eighth Notes

369
Track 57

94   The Total Jazz Drummer

Three-Note Groupings: Triplets

Three-Note Groupings: Sixteenth Notes

Four-Note Groupings

Stickings:
1. RLRL
2. LRLR
3. RRLL
4. LLRR
5. RLRR
6. LRLL
7. RLLR RLLR
8. LRRL LRRL
9. RRLR LLRL
10. LLRL RRLR

Four-Note Groupings: Eighth Notes

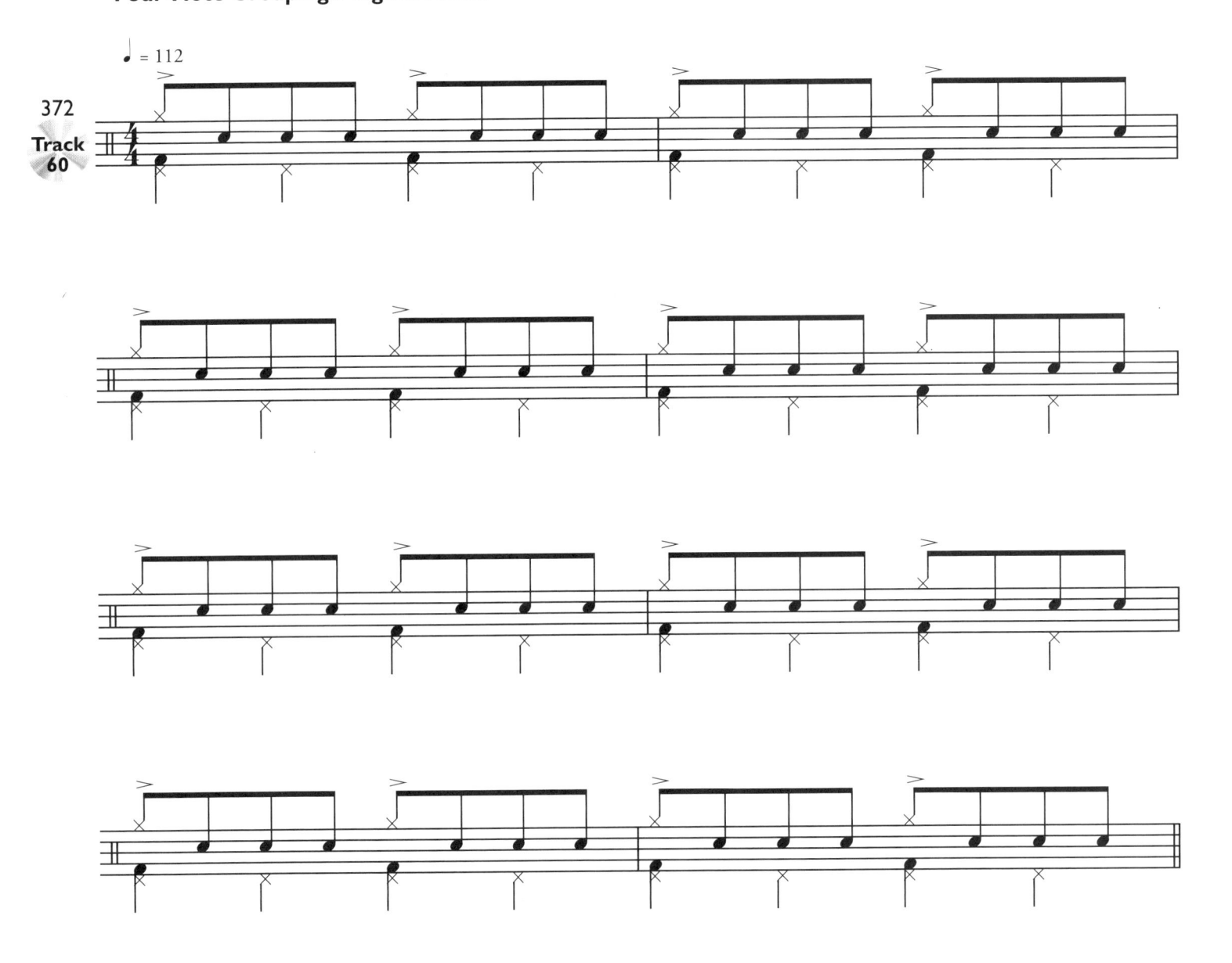

Four-Note Groupings: Triplets

Four-Note Groupings: Sixteenth Notes

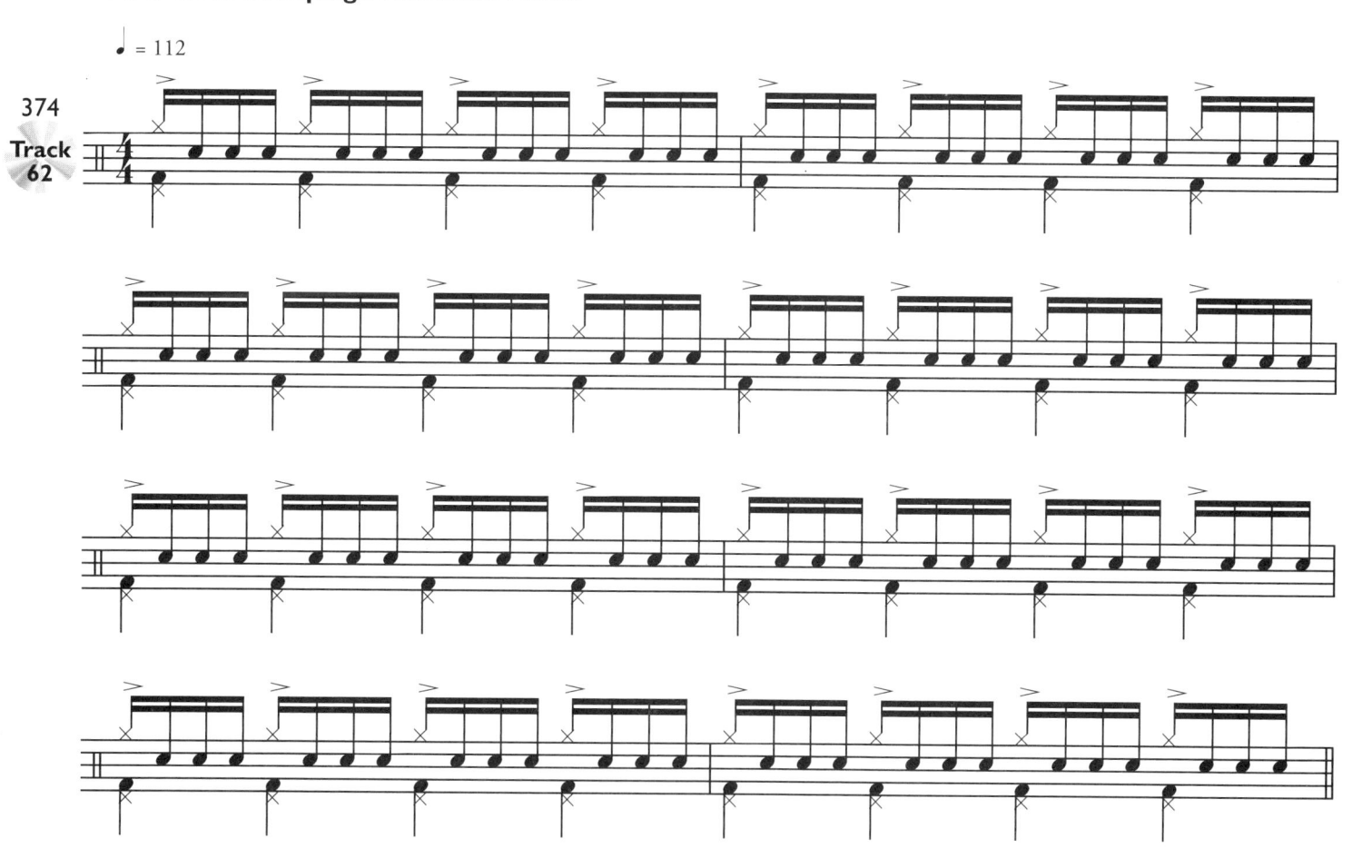

The Total Jazz Drummer

Five-Note Groupings

Stickings:
1. RLRLR LRLRL
2. LRLRL RLRLR
3. RLRLL
4. LRLRR
5. RRLLR LLRRL
6. LLRRL RRLLR
7. RRLLR RLLRR LLRRL LRRLL
8. LLRRL LRRLL RRLLR RLLRR
9. RLLRL
10. LRRLR

Five-Note Groupings: Eighth Notes

98 The Total Jazz Drummer

Five-Note Groupings: Triplets

Five-Note Groupings: Sixteenth Notes

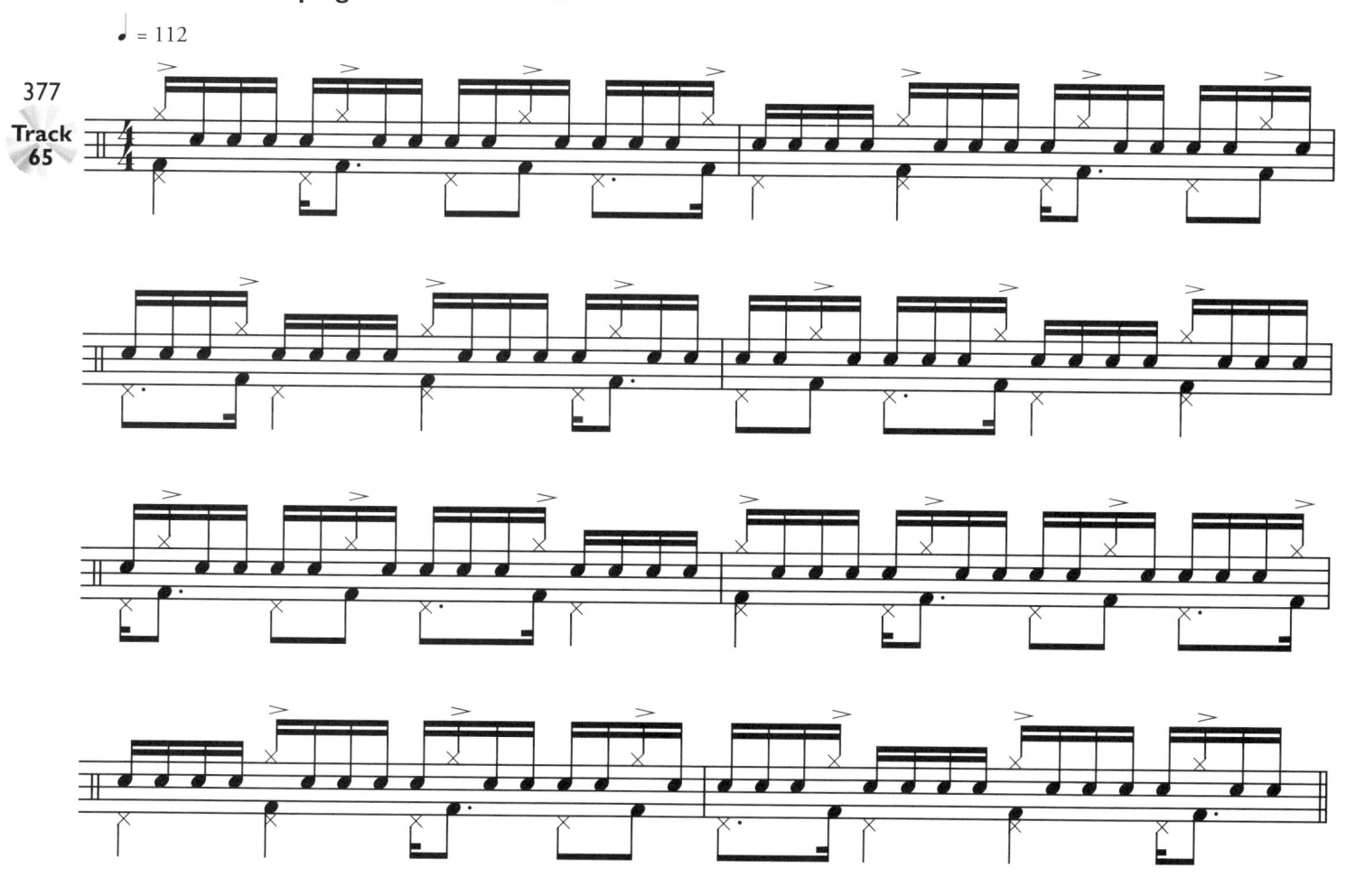

Seven-Note Groupings

Stickings:

1. RLRLRLR LRLRLRL
2. LRLRLRL RLRLRLR
3. RLRLRLL
4. LRLRLRR
5. RRLLRRL
6. LLRRLLR
7. RRLLRRL LRRLLRR LLRRLLR RLLRRLL
8. LLRRLLR RLLRRLL RRLLRRL LRRLLRR
9. RLLRLRL
10. LRRLRLR

Seven-Note Groupings: Eighth Notes

100 The Total Jazz Drummer

Seven-Note Groupings: Triplets

Seven-Note Groupings: Sixteenth Notes

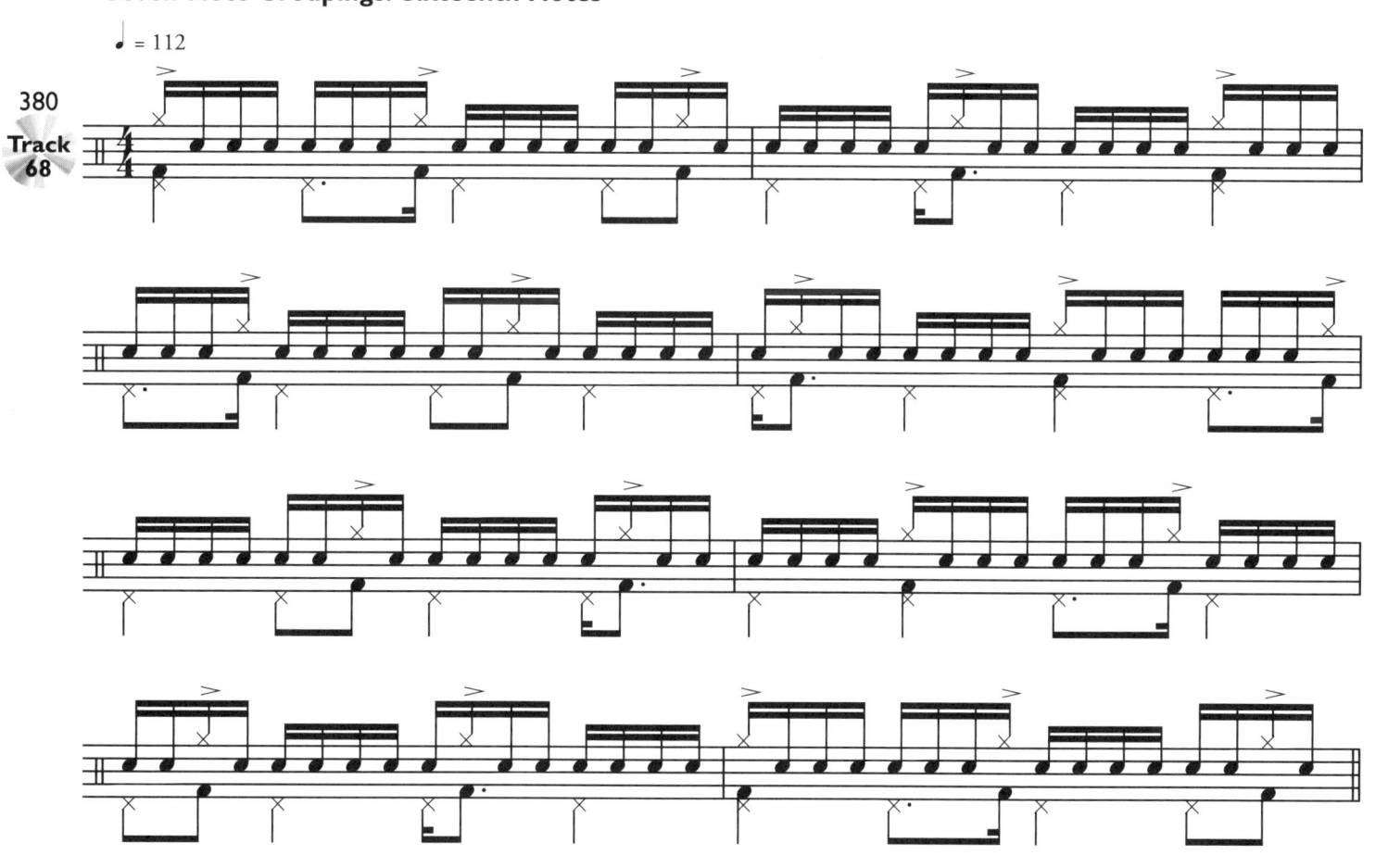

Linear Phrasing with the Ride Cymbal

The following pages have eighth notes, triplets and sixteenth notes grouped in threes, fours, fives and sevens. For this section, play the exercises with the different ride cymbal patterns given. Practice in two variations:

1. Play the "R" sticking on your bass drum and the "L" sticking on your snare drum.

2. Play the "R" sticking on your hi-hat foot and the "L" sticking on your snare drum.

Three-Note Groupings

Stickings:
1. RLL
2. LRR
3. LLR
4. RRL
5. RRR LLL
6. LLL RRR

Pattern 1

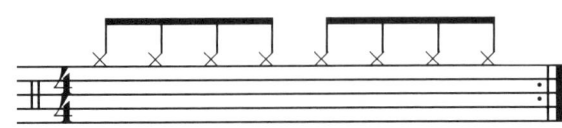

Pattern 2

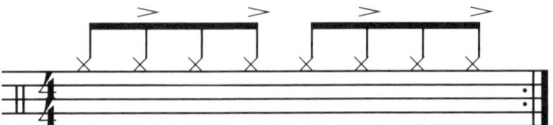

Pattern 3

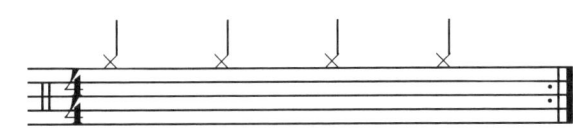

Pattern 4

Pattern 5

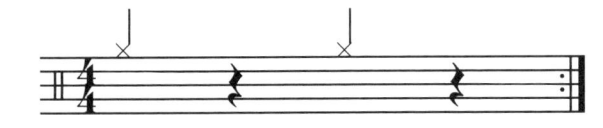

Pattern 6

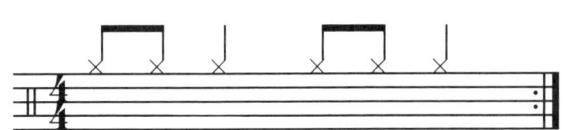

Pattern 7

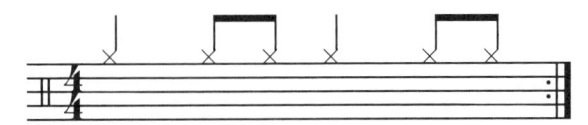

Three-Note Groupings: Eighth Notes

Three-Note Groupings: Triplets

Three-Note Groupings: Sixteenth Notes

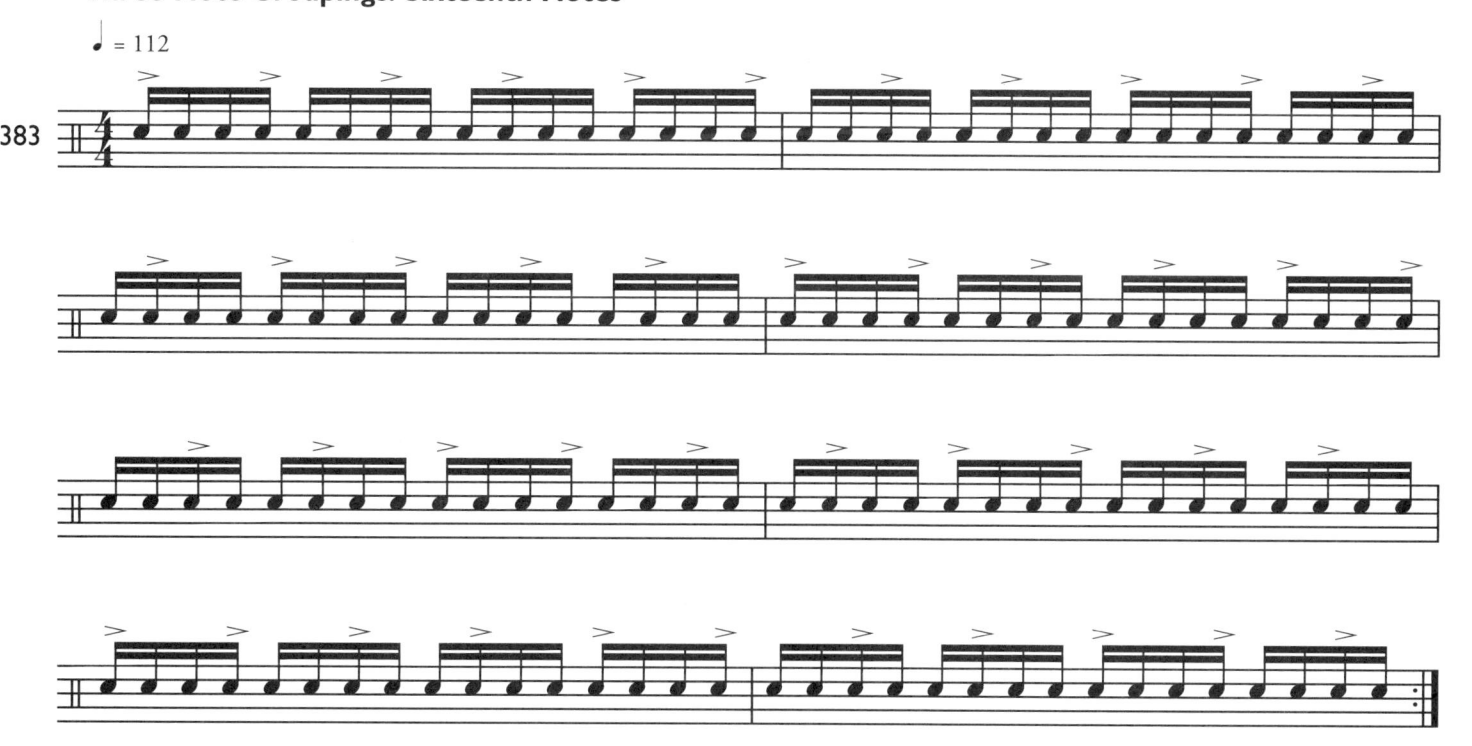

The Total Jazz Drummer

Four-Note Groupings

Stickings:

1. RRLL
2. LLRR
3. RLRR
4. LRLL

Play each of the following cymbal patterns with the note groupings on page 105.

Pattern 1

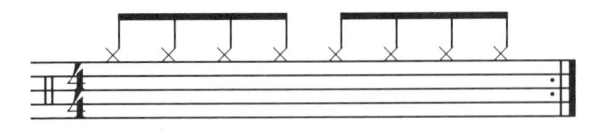

Pattern 2

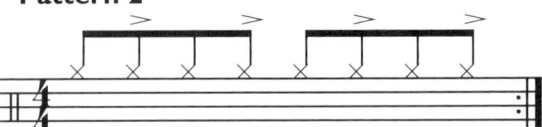

Pattern 3

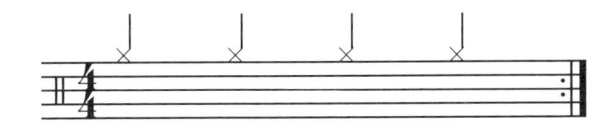

Pattern 4

Pattern 5

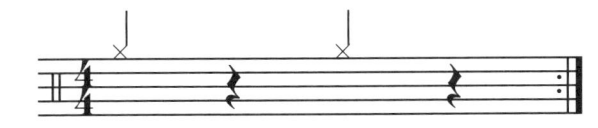

Pattern 6

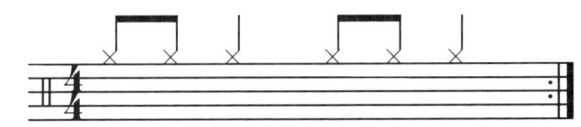

Pattern 7

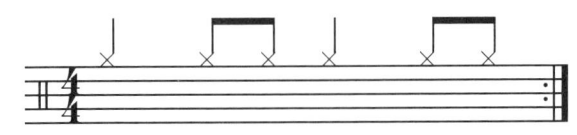

Four-Note Groupings: Eighth Notes

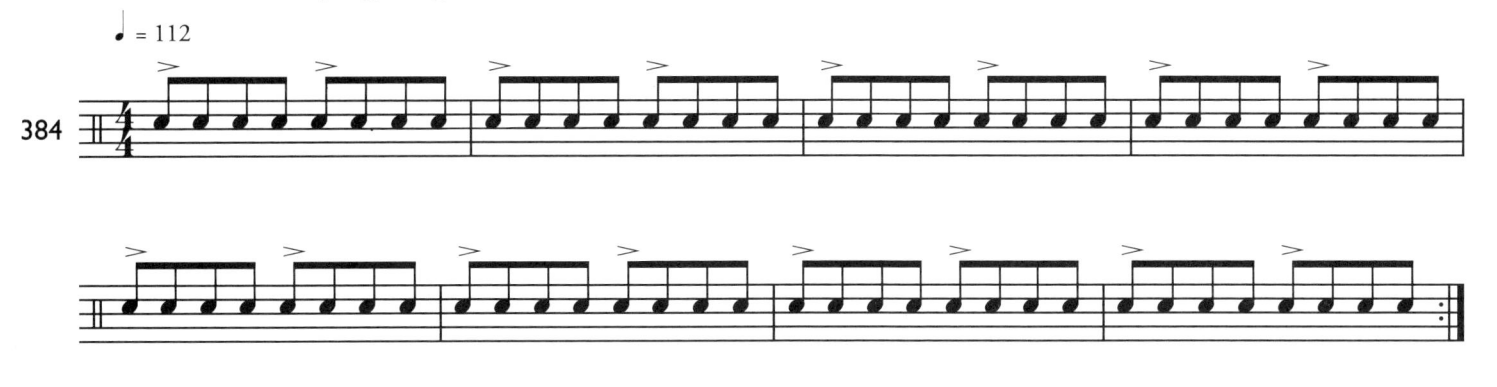

Four-Note Groupings: Triplets

Four-Note Groupings: Sixteenth Notes

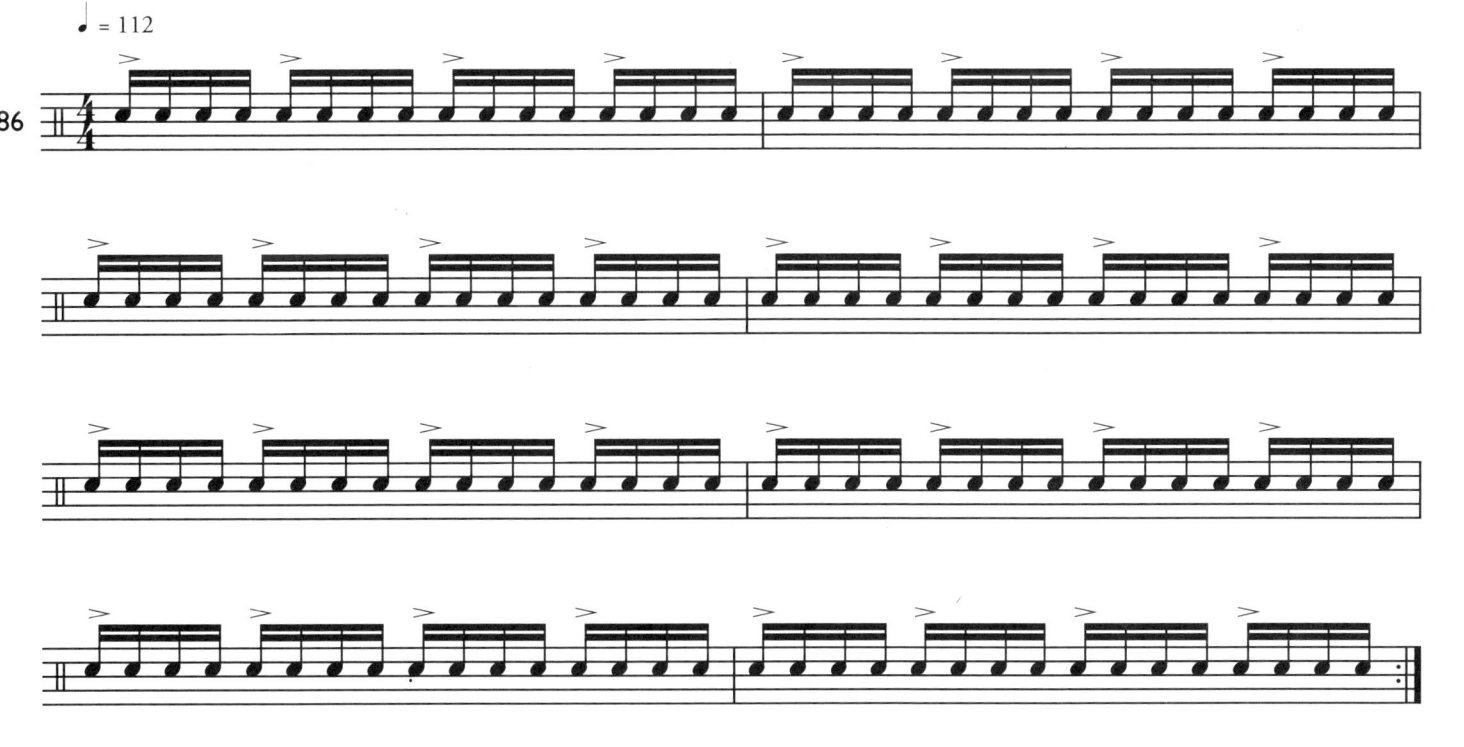

The Total Jazz Drummer

Five-Note Groupings

Stickings;
1. RLRLL
2. LRLRR
3. RLLRL
4. LRRLR
5. RRLLR LLRRL
6. LLRRL RRLLR

Play each of the following cymbal patterns with the note groupings on page 107.

Pattern 1

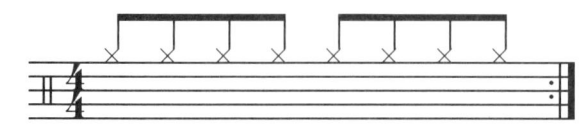

Pattern 2

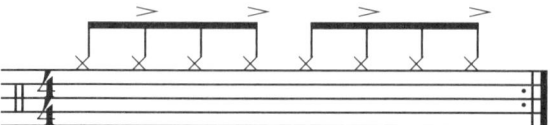

Pattern 3

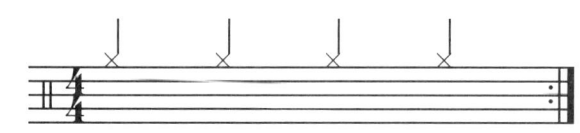

Pattern 4

Pattern 5

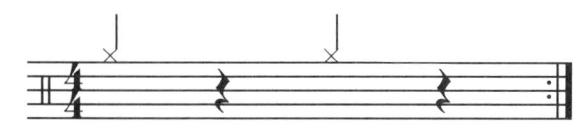

Pattern 6

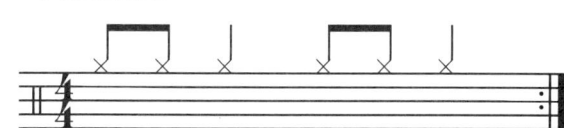

Pattern 7

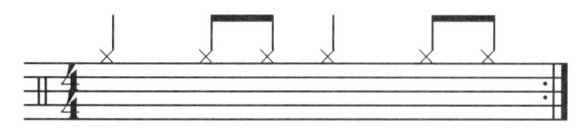

Five-Note Groupings: Eighth Notes

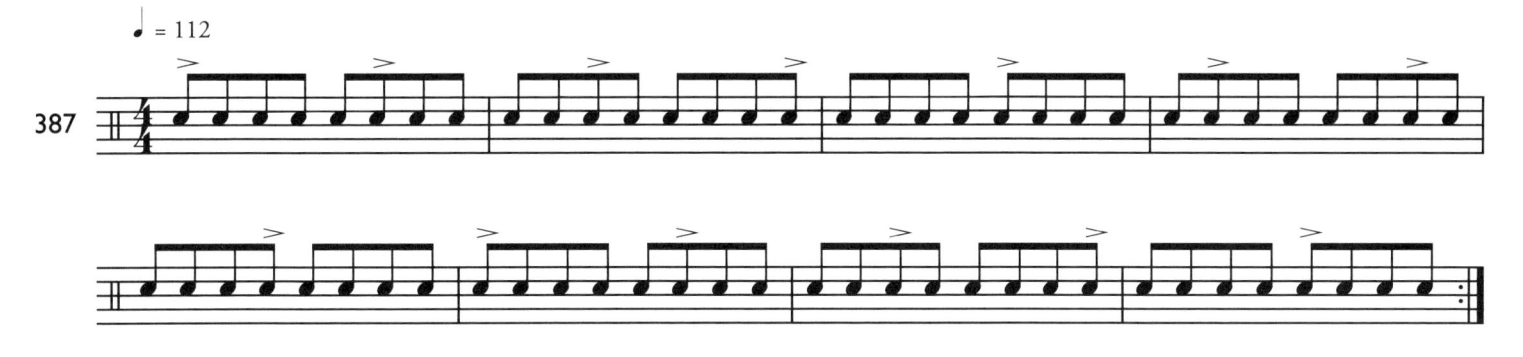

Five-Note Groupings: Triplets

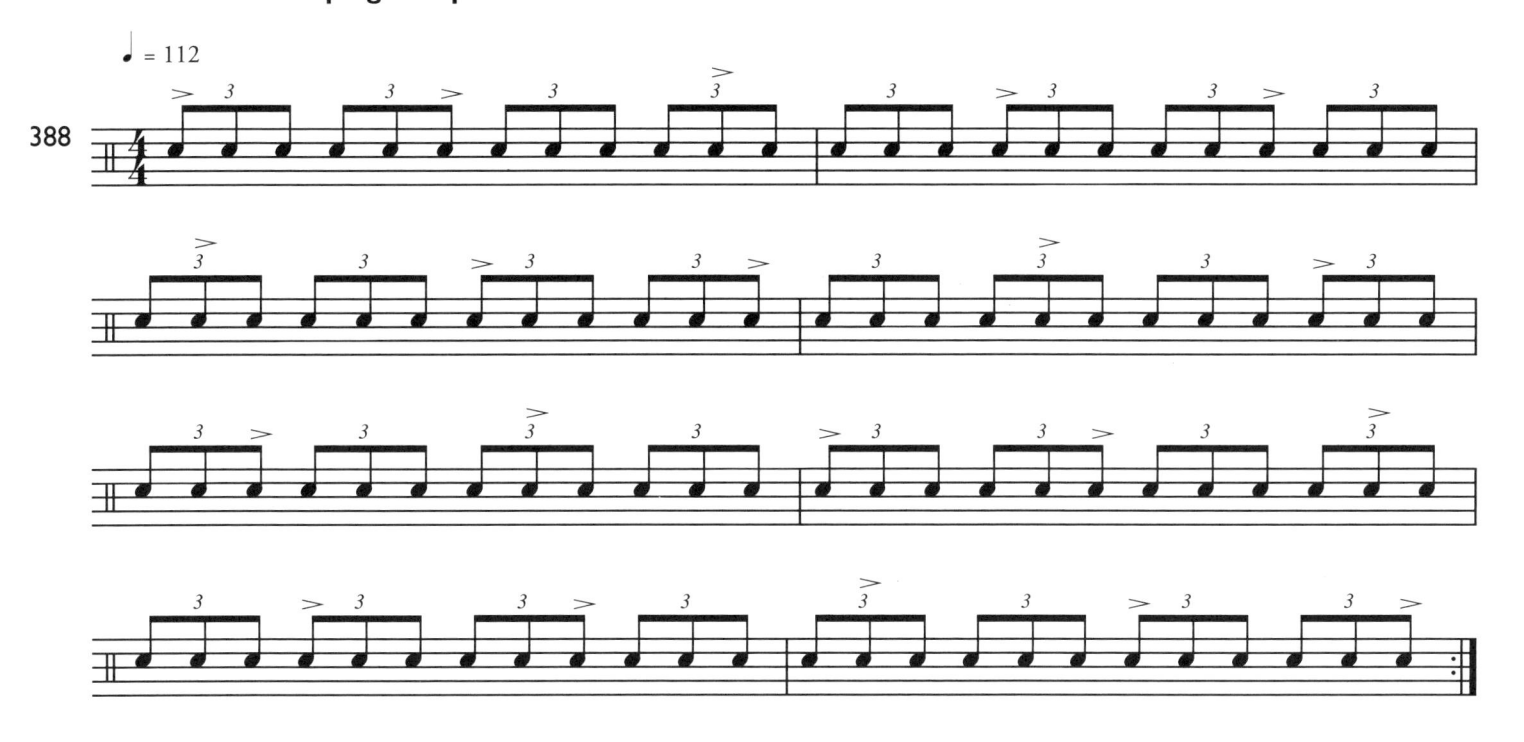

Five-Note Groupings: Sixteenth Notes

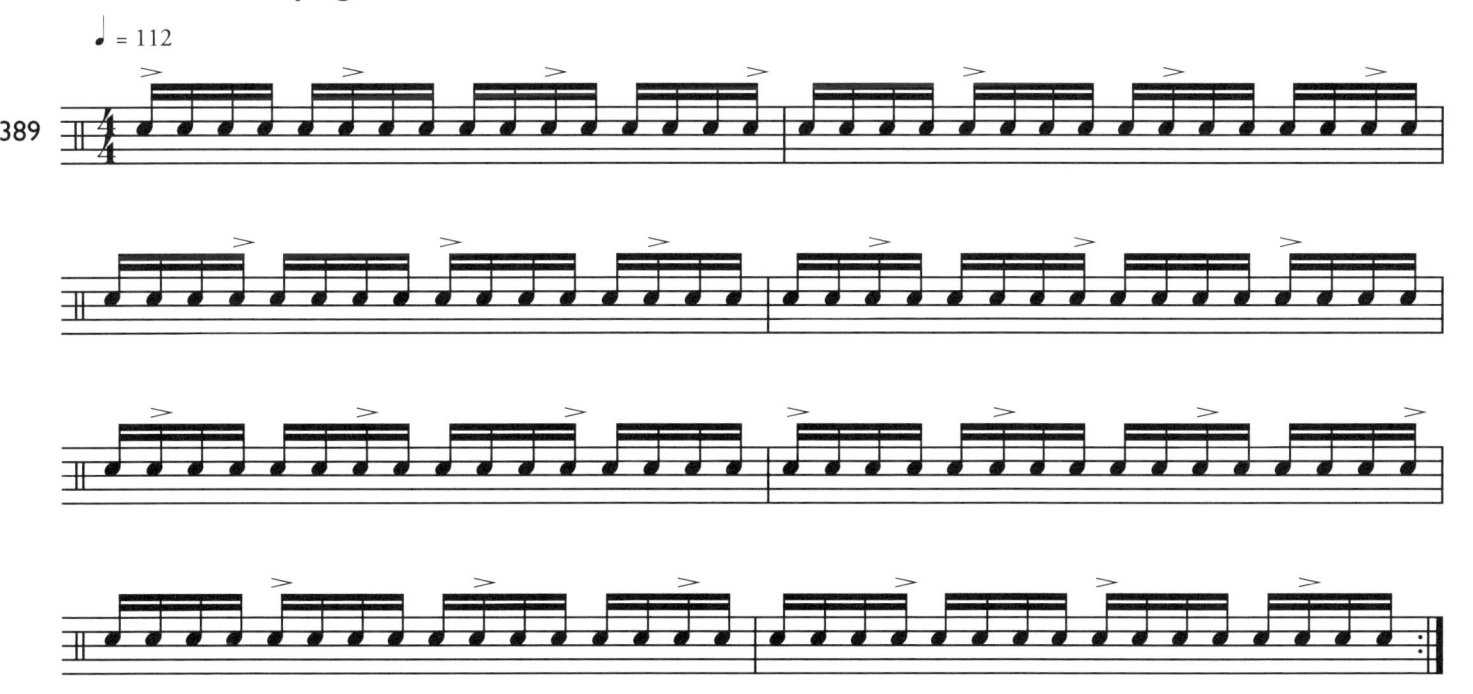

Seven-Note Groupings

Stickings:
1. RLRLRLL
2. LRLRLRR
3. RLLRLRL
4. LRRLRLR
5. RLRLLRL
6. LRLRRLR
7. RRLLRRL RRLLRRL
8. LLRRLLR LLRRLLR

Pattern 1

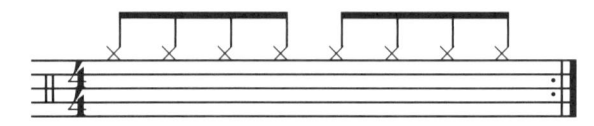

Pattern 2

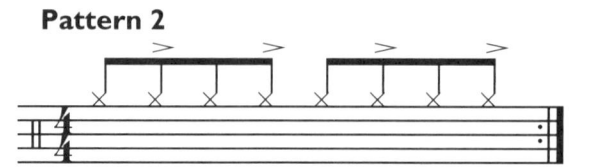

Pattern 3

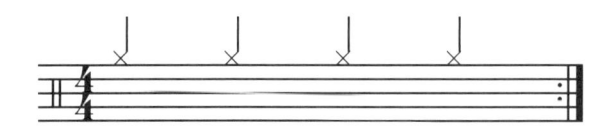

Pattern 4

Pattern 5

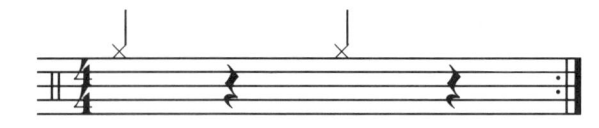

Pattern 6

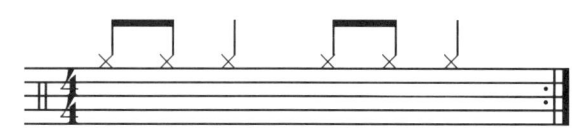

Pattern 7

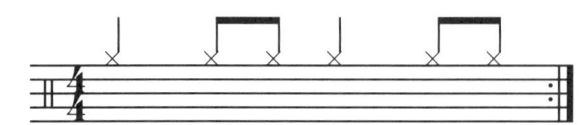

108 The Total Jazz Drummer

Seven-Note Groupings: Eighth Notes

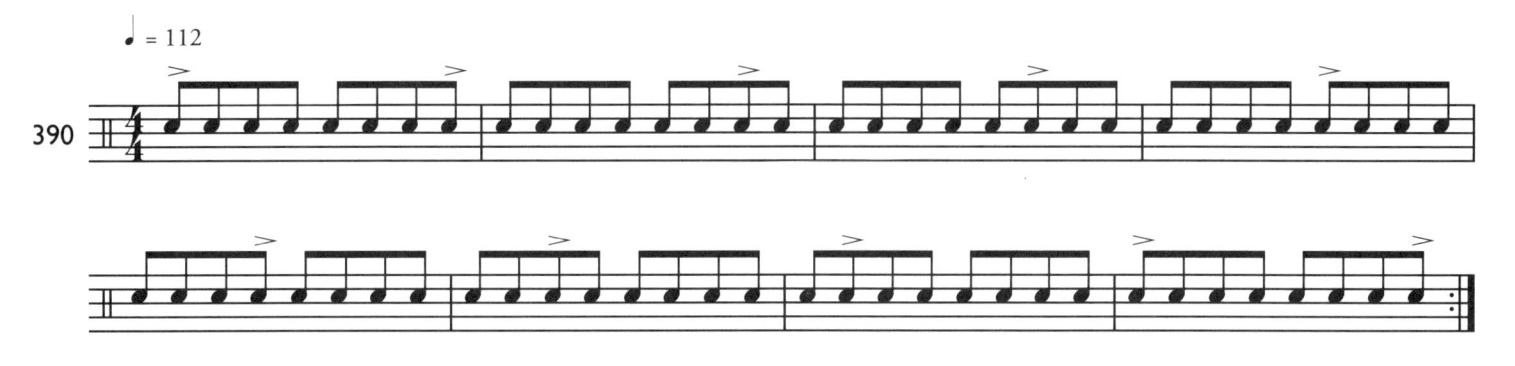

Seven-Note Groupings: Triplets

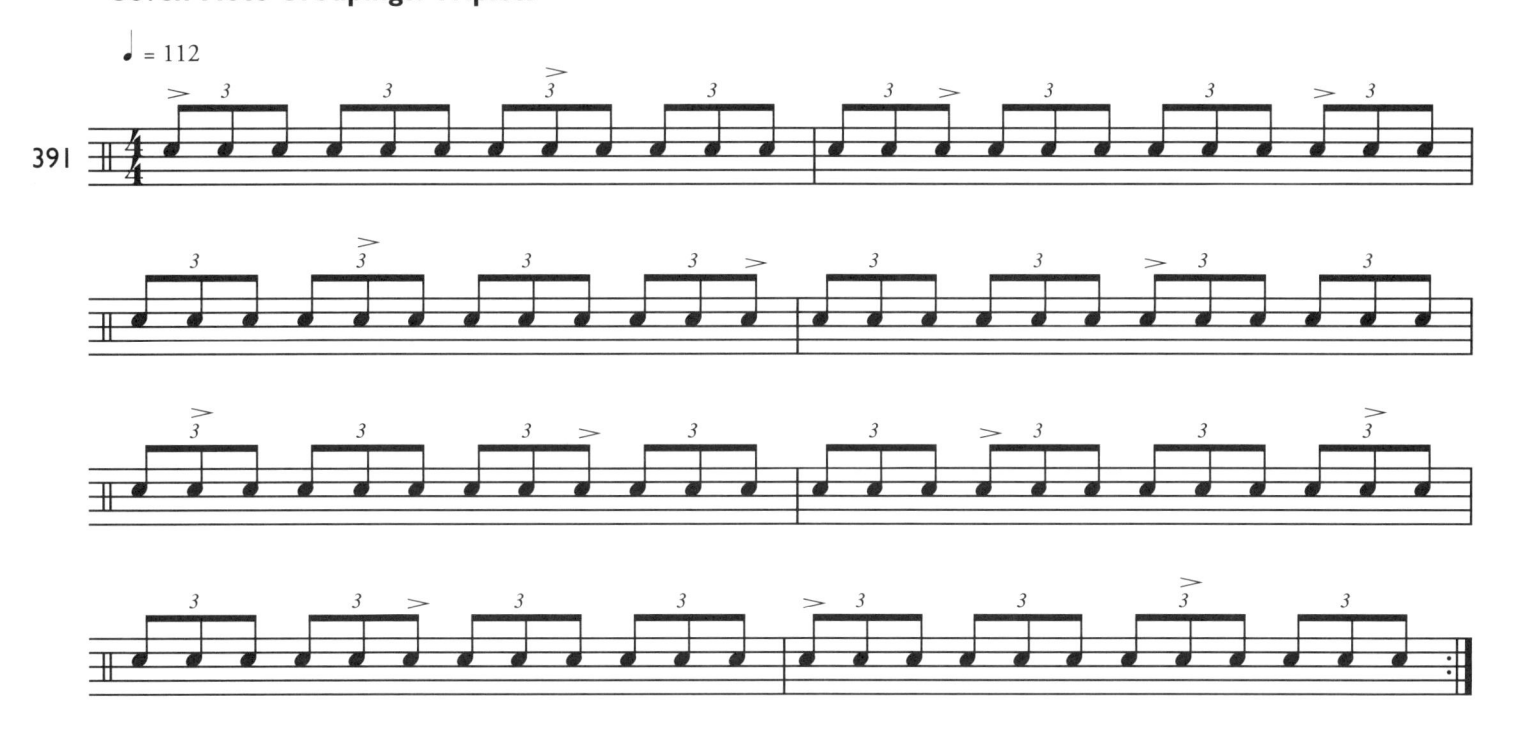

Seven-Note Groupings: Sixteenth Notes

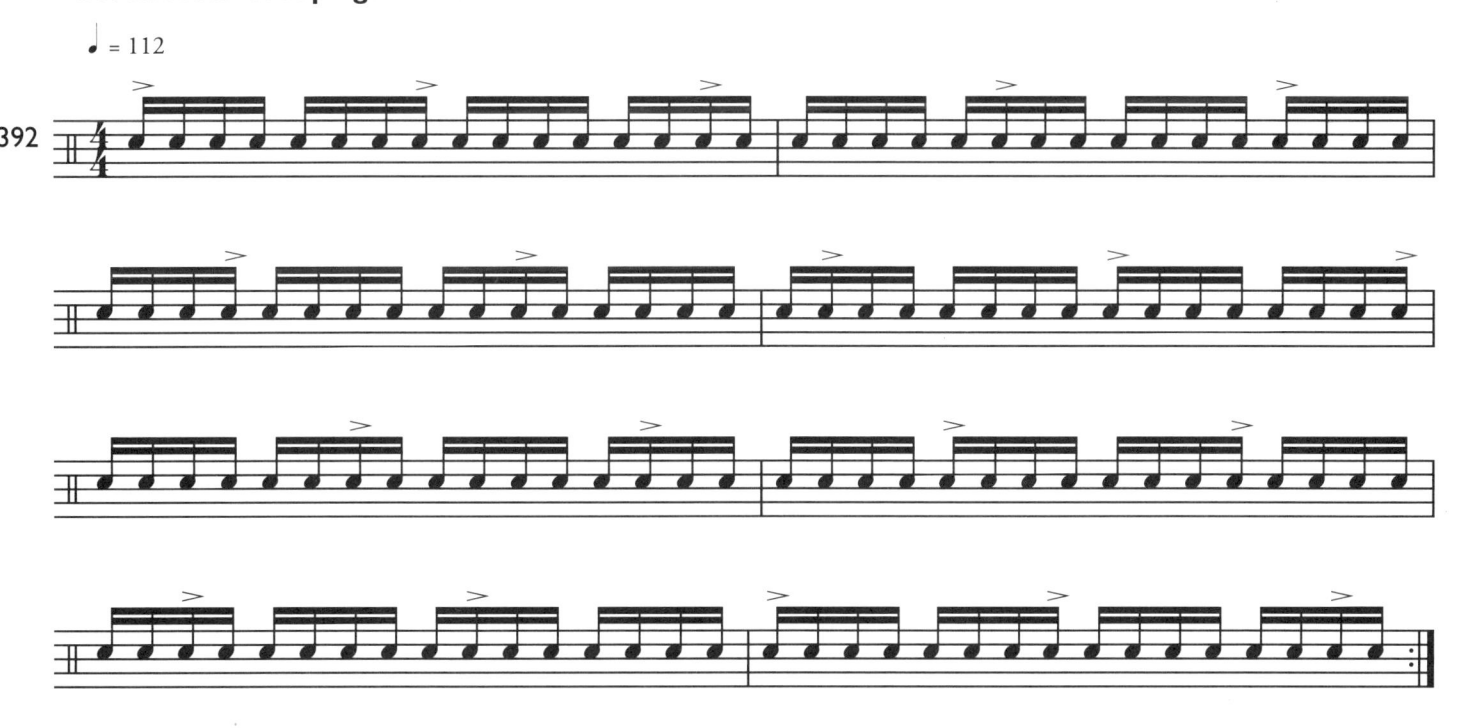

The Total Jazz Drummer

Chapter 10: Odd Time Meters

Odd time meters typically refer to all time signatures other than 4/4. Playing in odd time meters can be very challenging at first, mainly because a lifetime of listening to Western music does not accustom us to hearing this type of rhythm. One of the first odd time hits in jazz was the tune "Take Five" composed by Paul Desmond and recorded by the Dave Brubeck group in 1959. Brubeck's album *Time Out* included this hit along with other odd time jazz songs and featured the great drummer Joe Morello. In contemporary jazz, drummers are expected to be well-versed playing in different meters.

The best way to approach playing odd meters is to break up the measure into smaller components. For instance, a 7/4 measure can be looked at as a bar of 4/4 plus a bar of 3/4. A bar of 5/4 can be looked at as a bar of 3/4 plus a bar of 2/4 or just a bar of 4/4 with an extra beat at the end. There are multiple ways of breaking it down, so don't get used to playing a 7/4 Latin beat in just 4/4 and 3/4, for example.

Odd Time Exercises

The following exercises feature various odd meter rhythms that should be practiced at different tempos.

$\frac{5}{4}$ Swing

The following exercises are $\frac{5}{4}$ swing rhythms, as defined by the ride cymbal pattern. They should be practiced at different tempos.

5/4 Latin

The following exercises are 5/4 Latin-esque rhythms, as defined by the clave and ride cymbal patterns. You can play the cymbal patterns with the ride cymbal as written or you can use the bell of the ride cymbal. Practice the exercises at different tempos.

112   The Total Jazz Drummer

7/4 Swing

The following exercises are 7/4 swing rhythms, as defined by the ride cymbal pattern, and should be practiced at different tempos.

7/4 Latin

The following exercises are 7/4 Latin-esque rhythms, as defined by the clave and ride cymbal patterns. You can play the cymbal patterns with the ride cymbal as written or you can use the bell of the ride cymbal. Practice the exercises at different tempos.

114 The Total Jazz Drummer

Chapter 11: Rhythmic Grouping

In most Western music, we're used to hearing quarter notes, eighth notes, triplets and sixteenth notes. However, just as you can play two, three or four notes to one beat, you can also play five notes to a beat, or even seven notes to a beat. *Rhythmic grouping* has to do with how many notes you can play per beat, and is a way to expand your knowledge of rhythm and the possibilities of what else you can play on the drums.

The following exercise takes you through rhythmic groupings of two to eight notes and back down to two. Practice the following exercise using the following four stickings:

1. RLRLRLRL, etc.
2. LRLRLRLR, etc.
3. RRLLRRLL, etc.
4. LLRRLLRR, etc.

Chapter 12: Polyrhythms

A *polyrhythm* literally means "many rhythms." In this context, a polyrhythm is when two or more rhythms are played simultaneously. We can also look at a polyrhythm as two different meters (time signatures) played against each other. You've already played one of the most common polyrhythmic ratios: 2 against 3 (2:3) or 3 against 2 (3:2).

Below are some polyrhythmic ratios written in three different ways:

- A shows the subdivisions and relation of the rhythms to each other
- B shows the two rhythms against each other
- C shows how the polyrhythmic ratio is typically written in music

In some of the examples, the rhythm is only written in two ways (A and C). In these cases, the way the polyrhythm is usually written (C) is also the clearest way to show the two rhythms against each other.

On the CD, each rhythm is played for four measures, regardless of whether two or three different notations are shown.

Note: The rhythms notated are not to be played according to the drumset legend, but rather are meant to display their relationship to each other. You should first use your hands to play the rhythms against each other and then experiment with various combinations using all your limbs.

Polyrhythmic Ratios

2 against 3 (2:3)

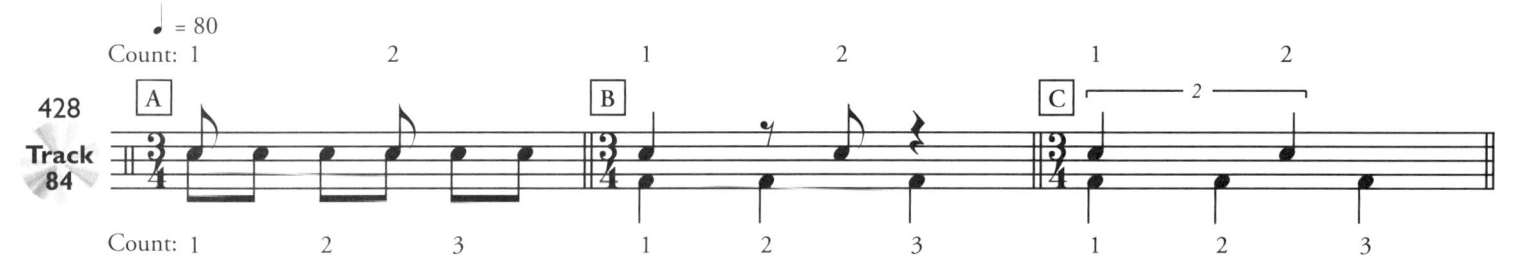

3 against 2 (3:2)

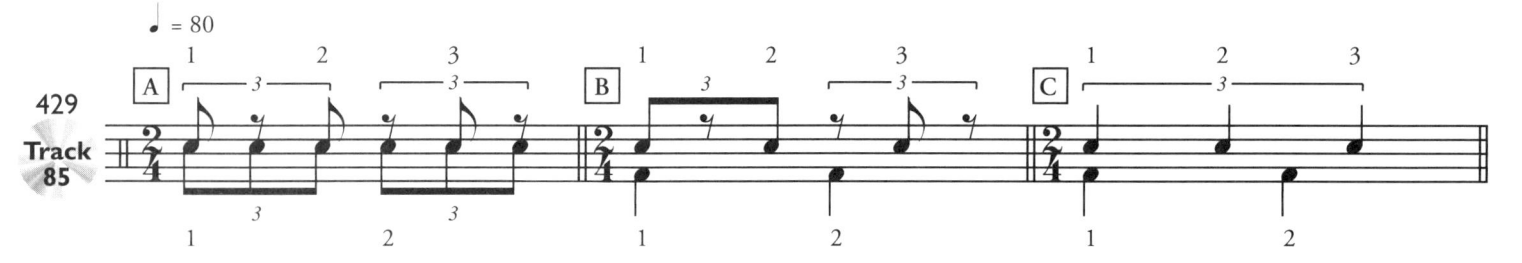

3 against 4 (3:4)

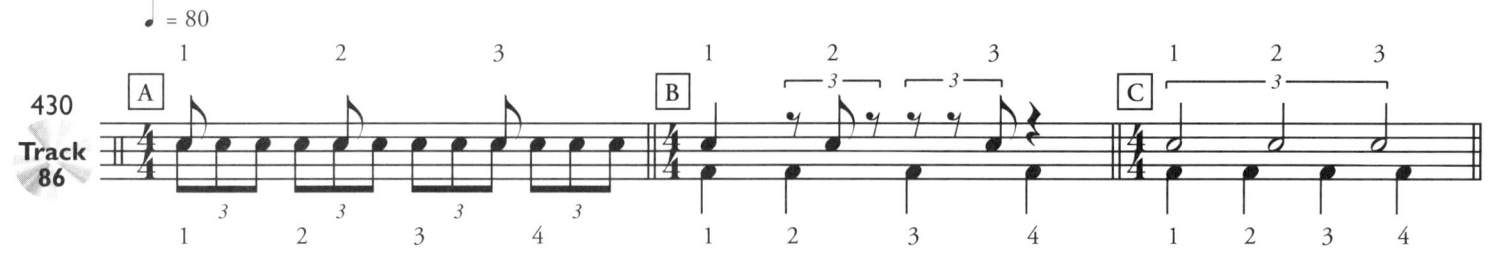

4 against 3 (4:3)

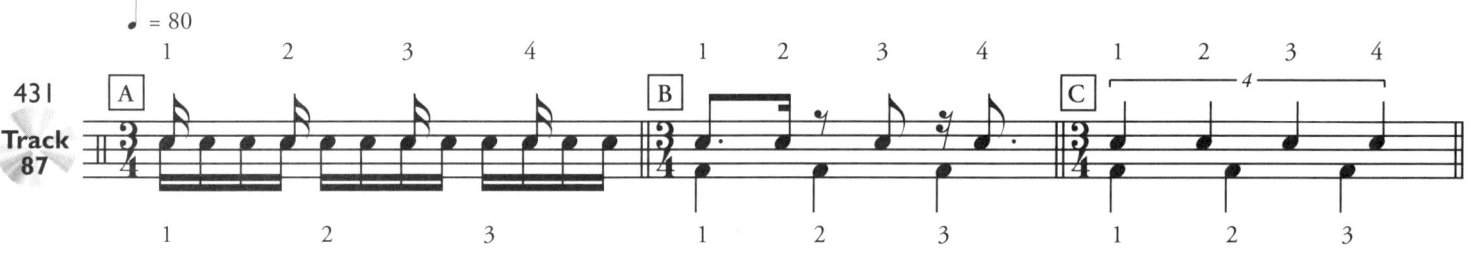

116   The Total Jazz Drummer

4 against 5 (4:5)

5 against 4 (5:4)

2 against 5 (2:5)

5 against 2 (5:2)

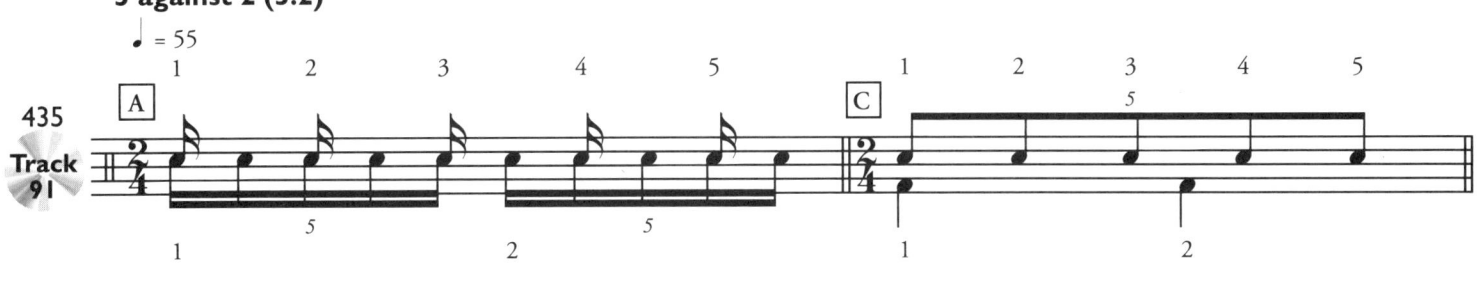

3 against 5 (3:5)

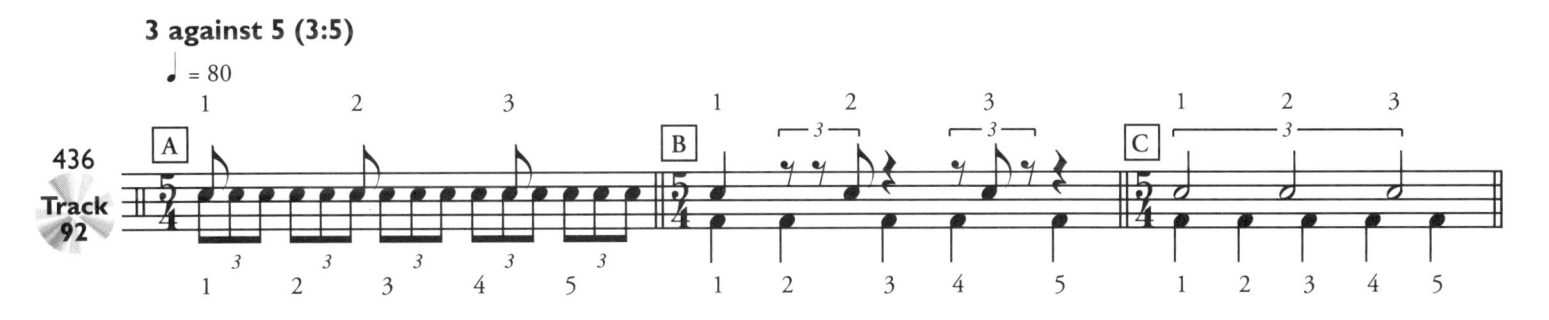

5 against 3 (5:3)

The Total Jazz Drummer

4 against 7 (4:7)

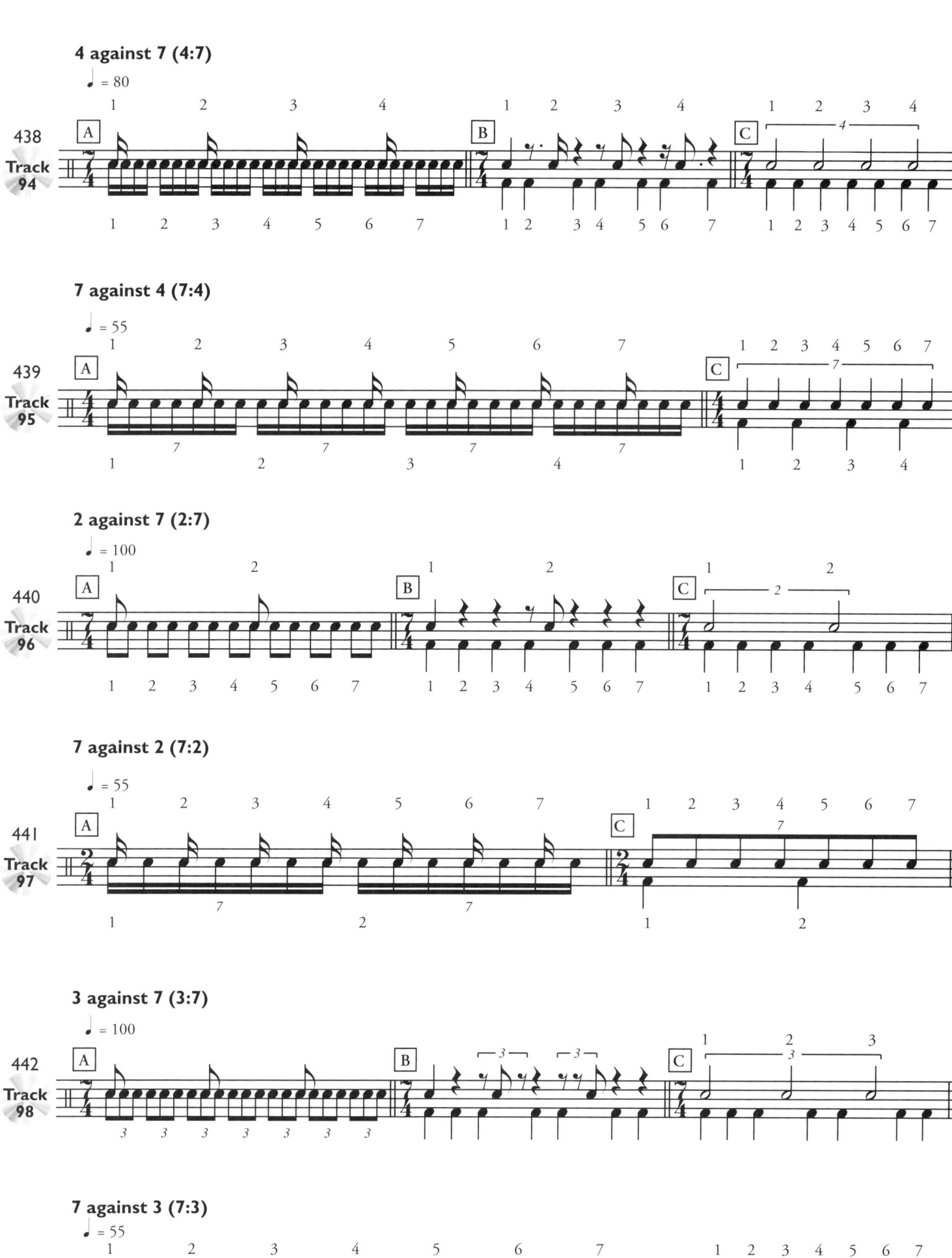

♩ = 80

438 Track 94

7 against 4 (7:4)

♩ = 55

439 Track 95

2 against 7 (2:7)

♩ = 100

440 Track 96

7 against 2 (7:2)

♩ = 55

441 Track 97

3 against 7 (3:7)

♩ = 100

442 Track 98

7 against 3 (7:3)

♩ = 55

443 Track 99

118   The Total Jazz Drummer

The Rhythm Table

You can take this concept further on your own by using the following rhythm table, which is designed for complete mastery of polyrhythms. It shows all possibilities of polyrhythmic ratios and variations. Practice playing different combinations of your hands against your feet. Some of them will be very easy, while others will be extremely difficult. The blacked out boxes are 1:1 ratios, meaning the rhythms are identical to each other.

Rhythm Table

	Hands											
Feet		1	2	3	4	5	6	7	8	9	10	11	etc.
	1	■											
	2		■										
	3			■									
	4				■								
	5					■							
	6						■						
	7							■					
	8								■				
	9									■			
	10										■		
	11											■	
	etc.												■

Art Blakey (1919–1990). "Buhaina" (as he is known) was one of the founding fathers of the jazz drumming language. Early in his career, Blakey played with some of the most prominent names in jazz, including Billy Eckstine, Bud Powell, Miles Davis and Thelonious Monk. As leader of the Jazz Messengers for over 30 years, he helped launch the careers of dozens of well-known jazz musicians. His legacy is still felt today in the hard bop sounds of mainstream jazz.

Courtesy of the Institute of Jazz Studies/Rutgers University

The Total Jazz Drummer

Chapter 13: Polyrhythmic Limbs

Polyrhythmic limbs is a concept having to do with the numerous ways you can apply polyrhythms to the drumset. It ties together the previous chapters of linear phrasing and polyrhythmic ratios and applies those concepts to the drumset. Some of the masters who use this concept to great extent are Tony Williams, Jeff "Tain" Watts, Bill Stewart, Dan Weiss, Ari Hoening and a host of other up-and-coming jazz drummers.

There are a couple of ways to approach this:

1. **Note groupings**—Refer to the linear phrasing section (page 84). For example, you can play a grouping of four quarter notes in the feet against a grouping of three eighth notes in the hands.

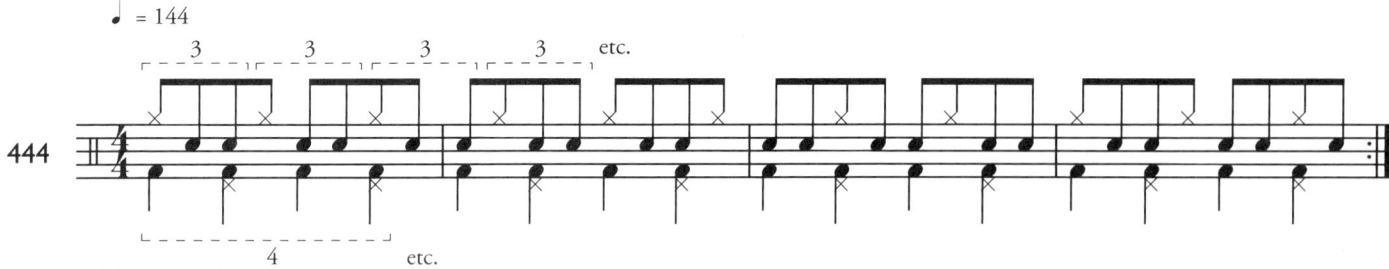

Now employ the swing pattern.

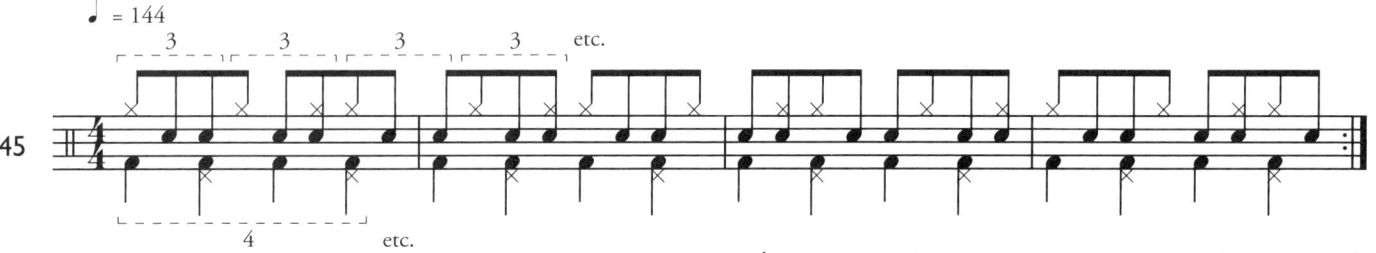

Here's another example where you can play a grouping of four quarter notes on the ride cymbal, three eighth notes on the bass drum and five eighth notes on the snare (playing only beats 1 and 3 of the five grouping).

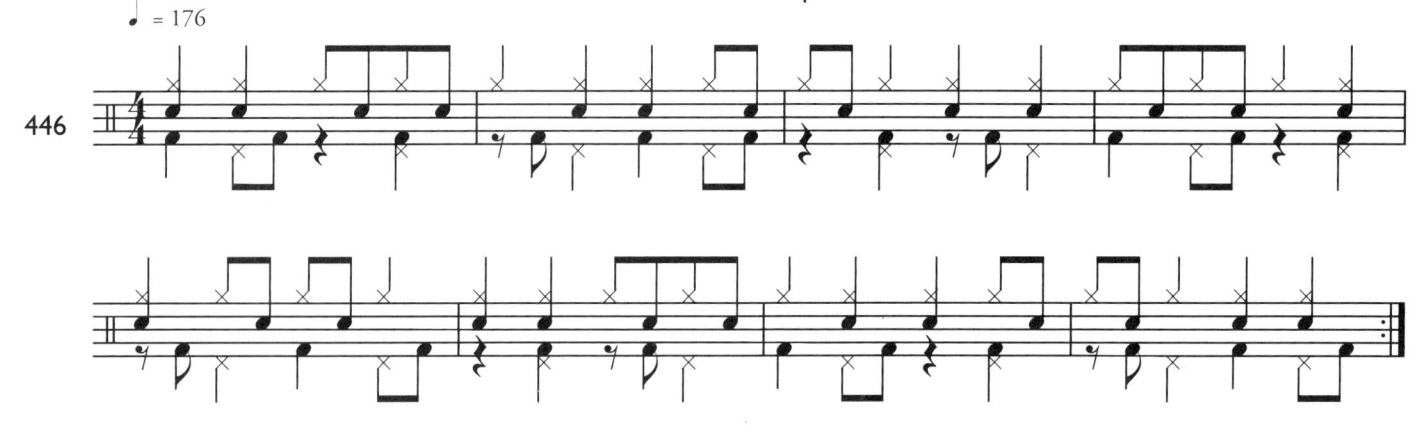

Now, employ the swing pattern.

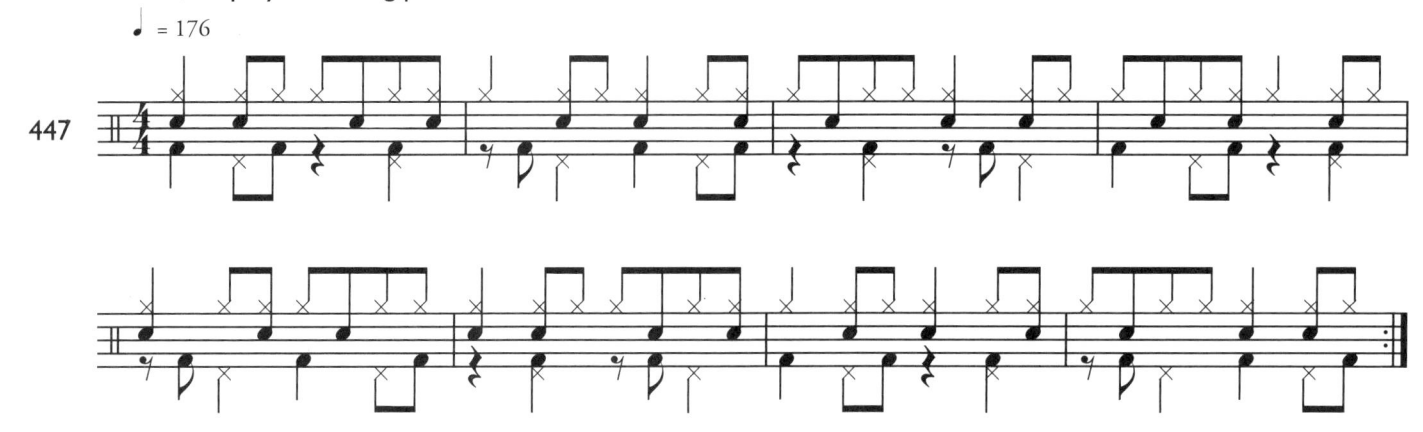

2. **Superimposing**—*Superimposing* is playing two or more meters simultaneously and having them both start together on beat one every measure, similar to the chapter on polyrhythmic ratios. For example, a basic superimposition we've practiced throughout the book is playing 4/4 in your hands and 3/4 in your feet.

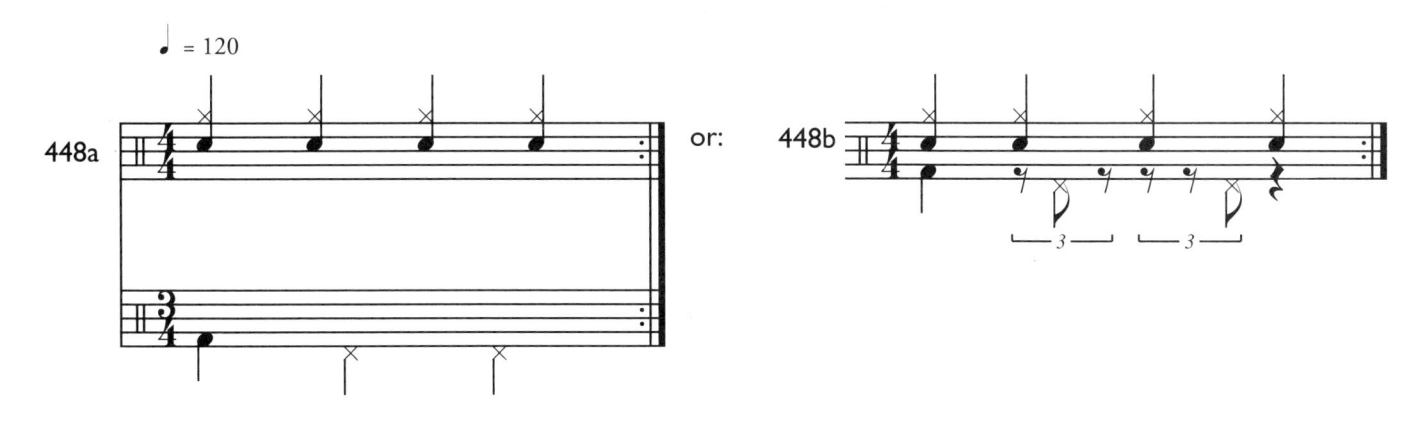

Now employ the swing pattern.

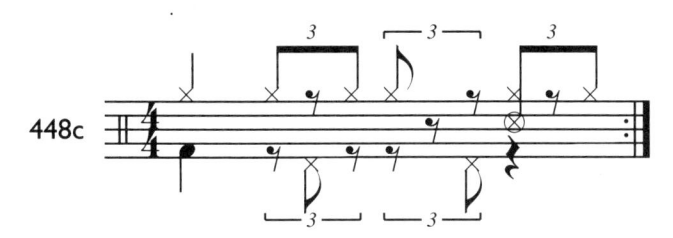

Here's another example where you can play a measure of 5/4 in your hands, while playing a measure of 4/4 in your feet.

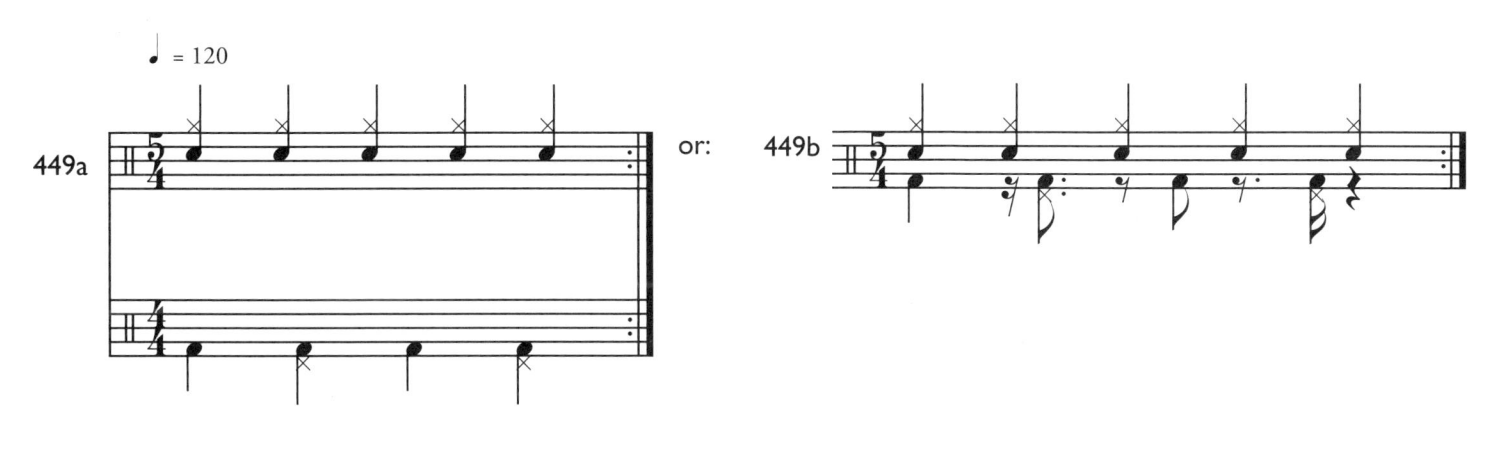

Now employ the swing pattern.

There are endless possibilities to this concept, and I hope that these chapters on polyrhythms will inspire you to create your own ideas and applications of this approach to jazz drumming. After all, when all is said and done, jazz is about the creative spirit within.

Appendix
Improvisation

Congratulations on completing *The Total Jazz Drummer*. That brings us to the one defining element that sets the great jazz drummers apart from the others: *improvisation*. Improvisation is an essential element of jazz music. Yes, there is a language, history and tradition to playing jazz, but once you've grasped that, jazz is ultimately about tapping into your creative spirit and being able to draw from all that you've learned in order to improvise. You should constantly be attempting to create new, fresh ideas and sounds in the practice room and on the bandstand. Let's break this down into three topics that will help you approach jazz as an improvisatory art form.

1. **Be Open**
   Jazz is really about all types of music. If you take a look at the development of jazz, it's evolved in the past 100 years to encompass various sub-genres. There is Dixieland, ragtime, New Orleans, Latin jazz, big band, bebop, hard bop, cool jazz, smooth jazz, fusion, avant-garde, acid jazz, *etc*. Through its history, jazz music has been very much influenced by its environment, society and socio-political climate. That is why it's understandable that jazz has been incorporating rap and hip-hop beats since the 1980s and, for the past 10 years, has also been influenced by electronic music. Whatever jazz you choose to play, checking out all types of music is essential to being a jazz drummer. Expose yourself to music from different cultures. Listen to operas, classical music, electronic music, *etc*. The more you stay open to, the more music you can draw from when improvising.

2. **Explore Sound**
   Don't approach the drums as just a rhythmical instrument. Make use of the different *timbres* (tone qualities) and sounds that you can pull from the entire drumset. Try playing on the rims of drums; play on the cymbal stands; try different sticks. A drummer will usually play with sticks, but may also use brushes, mallets, hands or any variety of "multi-rod" sticks. Sing while playing. Try tuning your drums to certain pitches and make up melodies. There are endless possibilities to the sound you can get from your drums. It's all about taking yourself "out of the box" to discover new ways of playing.

3. **Develop Your Own Voice on the Drums**
   The role of the drummer is to keep time and to play for the music. Learning the fundamentals and language that's been laid out by the masters is the first step in becoming a jazz drummer. You now have to make this music yours, meaning, you have to push yourself to develop your own style and sound on the drums.

Professional Advice

I thought it would be best if I shared some of my experiences with you, mainly because the one thing that music camps, teachers, colleges, *etc.* forget to tell you is that music *is* a business. For those of you thinking of becoming a professional musician, there are many things to consider and to remember.

- **Love music first and foremost.** Don't go into music thinking you're going to become a star. That doesn't mean you will fail, it just means it's very difficult to reach the topmost level. So, if that's your priority, the odds are not in your favor.

- **Don't just be a drummer, be a musician.** Learn to play some piano or guitar, or perhaps some other melodic instrument. Know your scales, intervals and chords. Being able to hear these things allows you to hear all of music and not just rhythm. It also gives you the tools to compose. (For a good introduction to learning jazz piano, check out *Beginning Jazz Keyboard* by Noah Baerman; National Guitar Workshop/Alfred #22619.)

- **Stay healthy.** What you put into your body and mind will affect your performance on your instrument. Remember that the drums are an extension of you. You are the real instrument!

- **Develop a warm-up and practice routine** and schedule it into your day.

- **Music is a business,** and being able to play the heck out of the drums is only half the battle. These are some points to keep in mind as a performing musician:
  - Have a strong ability to read and interpret music charts.
  - Have a good attitude.
  - Identify what the bandleader (your employer) wants from you.
  - Presentation is key. How you look affects your work, and how your drums look reflects on you as well.
  - Be on time for everything, no matter how much money it pays. If you agree to do a gig, give it your 100% professional attention.

Outro

I hope that by going through this book you've discovered jazz drumming to be fun, challenging and exciting. This book is by no means the end to your jazz drumming education. You should always be hungry for more education and information; check out other instructional books, study with different teachers, listen to recordings, go hear live music, practice and play with other musicians. Your quest for learning new things should never end. Remember to always challenge yourself. That's the only way to grow as a musician. As I mentioned before, practicing means working on the things you can't do that well, not playing everything you already know. I hope that this book has inspired and motivated you and helped you develop your jazz drumming skills.

Listening Guide

Here's a list of some great, inspiring jazz recordings.

Artist	Recording	Record Label	Drummer
Rez Abbasi	Snake Charmer	Earthsounds	Danny Weiss
Alas No Axis	Splay	Winter & Winter	Jim Black
Julian "Cannonball" Adderley	Somethin' Else	Blue Note Records	Art Blakey
Julian "Cannonball" Adderley	Mercy, Mercy, Mercy	Capitol Records	Roy McCurdy
Louis Armstrong	The Complete California Concerts	Decca Records/Verve	Cozy Cole
Kenny Barron	Things Unseen	Verve Records	Victor Lewis
Kenny Barron	Lemuria-Seascape	Candid Records	Ben Riley
Count Basie	At Newport	Verve Records	Sonny Payne
Count Basie	April in Paris	Verve Records	Sonny Payne
Brian Blade Fellowship	self-titled	Blue Note Records	Brian Blade
Brian Blade Fellowship	Perceptual	Blue Note Records	Brian Blade
Art Blakey and The Jazz Messengers	Moanin'	Blue Note Records	Art Blakey
Art Blakey and The Jazz Messengers	Mosaic	Blue Note Records	Art Blakey
Art Blakey and The Jazz Messengers	Free For All	Blue Note Records	Art Blakey
Clifford Brown & Max Roach	self-titled	EmArcy Records/Verve	Max Roach
Clifford Brown & Max Roach	At Basin Street	EmArcy Records/Verve	Max Roach
Dave Brubeck	Take Five	Columbia Records	Joe Morello
Ornette Coleman	The Shape of Jazz to Come	Atlantic Records	Billy Higgins
Ornette Coleman	This is Our Music	Atlantic Records	Ed Blackwell
Steve Coleman & The Metrics	The Way of The Cipher	RCA Records	Gene Lake
John Coltrane	A Love Supreme	Impulse Records	Elvin Jones
John Coltrane	Giant Steps	Atlantic Records	Cobb/Humphries/Taylor
John Coltrane	Blue Train	Blue Note Records	"Philly" Joe Jones
Chick Corea	Now He Sings, Now He Sobs	Solid State	Roy Haynes
Chick Corea	Trio Music	ECM Records	Roy Haynes
Miles Davis	Round About Midnight	Columbia Records	"Philly" Joe Jones
Miles Davis	Kind of Blue	Columbia Records	Jimmy Cobb
Miles Davis	Miles Smiles	Columbia Records	Tony Williams
Miles Davis	Bitches Brew	Columbia Records	Lenny White/Jack DeJohnette

Artist	Album	Label	Drummer
Warren "Baby" Dodds	High Society	Blue Note Records	Warren "Baby" Dodds
Duke Ellington & His Orchestra	At Newport	Columbia Records	Sam Woodyard
Duke Ellington	Money Jungle	Blue Note Records	Max Roach
Duke Ellington & John Coltrane	self-titled	Impulse Records	Elvin Jones/Sam Woodyard
Ella Fitzgerald	Best of the Duke Ellington Songbook	Verve Records	Sam Woodyard/Alvin Stoller
Bill Frisell	East/West	Nonesuch Records	Kenny Wollesen
Stan Getz/Kenny Barron	People Time	Verve Records	Sax/piano (no drums)
Dizzy Gillespie	Dizzy's Diamonds	Verve Records	Various
Dizzy Gillespie/Charlie Parker	Town Hall, NYC, June 22, 1945	Uptown Jazz	"Big" Sid Catlett/Max Roach
Benny Goodman	Carnegie Hall Jazz Concert – 1938	Sony Music	Gene Krupa
Dexter Gordon	Go	Blue Note Records	Billy Higgins
Herbie Hancock	Empyrean Isles	Blue Note Records	Tony Williams
Herbie Hancock	Headhunters	Columbia Records	Harvey Mason
Tim Hagans	Animation-Imagination	Blue Notes Records	Billy Kilson
Coleman Hawkins	Jazz Tribune No. 52: The Indispensible Coleman Hawkins	RCA Records	Various
Roy Haynes	Out of the Afternoon	Verve Records	Roy Haynes
Joe Henderson	Inner Urge	Blue Note Records	Elvin Jones
Billie Holiday	Lady in Satin	Columbia Records	Osie Johnson
Zakir Hussain	Making Music	ECM Records	Zakir Hussain
Ahmad Jamal	But Not For Me: Live at the Pershing	Chess Records	Vernal Fournier
Keith Jarrett	The Mourning of a Star	Atlantic Records	Paul Motian
Keith Jarrett	Belonging	ECM Records	Jon Christensen
Keith Jarrett	Changeless	ECM Records	Jack DeJohnette
Keith Jarrett	Standards, Vol. 1	ECM Records	Jack DeJohnette
Antonio Carlos Jobim	The Man From Ipanema	Verve Records	Various
Elvin Jones	Live at the Lighthouse	Blue Note Records	Elvin Jones
Jo Jones	The Essential	Vanguard Records	"Papa" Jo Jones
Thad Jones-Mel Lewis Orchestra	Central Park North	Blue Note Records	Mel Lewis
Wayne Krantz	Greenwich Mean	Independent	Keith Carlock
Lifetime	Emergency	Polydor Records	Tony Williams
Lifetime	Ego	Polydor Records	Tony Williams
Charles Lloyd	A Night In Copenhagen	Blue Note Records	Sonship Theus

Artist	Album	Label	Drummer
Branford Marsalis	The Dark Keys	Columbia Records	Jeff "Tain" Watts
Wynton Marsalis	Black Codes (From The Underground)	Columbia Records	Jeff "Tain" Watts
Masada	Live in Sevilla	Tzadik	Joey Baron
John McLaughlin Trio	Live at The Royal Festival Hall	JMT/Polygram Records	Trilok Gurtu
Pat Metheny	Bright Size Life	ECM Records	Bob Moses
Charles Mingus	The Black Saint and the Sinner Lady	Impulse Records	Dannie Richmond
Charles Mingus	Town Hall Concert	Jazz Workshop	Dannie Richmond
Thelonious Monk Quartet	Misterioso	Riverside Records	Roy Haynes
Thelonious Monk Quartet	With John Coltrane at Carnegie Hall	Blue Note Records	Shadow Wilson
Charlie Parker	Bird at St. Nick's	Original Jazz Classics	Roy Haynes
Maceo Parker	Life on Planet Groove	Verve Records	Kenwood Dennard
Jean-Michel Pilc	Cardinal Points	Dreyfuss Records	Ari Hoenig
The Quintet	Jazz at Massey Hall	Debut Records	Max Roach
Buddy Rich	The Best of Buddy Rich	Pacific Records	Buddy Rich
Sonny Rollins	Saxophone Colossus	Prestige Records	Max Roach
Sonny Rollins	Night at the Village Vanguard	Blue Note Records	Pete LaRoca/Elvin Jones
John Scofield	Hand Jive	Blue Note Records	Bill Stewart
Wayne Shorter	Adam's Apple	Blue Note Records	Joe Chambers
Wayne Shorter	Schizophrenia	Blue Note Records	Joe Chambers
Zutty Singleton & His Orchestra	King Porter Stomp	Decca Records	Zutty Singleton
Bill Stewart	Telepathy	Blue Note Records	Bill Stewart
The Poll Winners	Exploring the Scene	OJC	Shelly Manne
Tower of Power	Back to Oakland	Warner Brothers Records	Dave Garibaldi
McCoy Tyner	The Real McCoy	Blue Note Records	Elvin Jones
McCoy Tyner	Inception	Impulse Records	Elvin Jones
Weather Report	I Sing The Body Electric	Columbia Records	Eric Gravatt
Chick Webb	Spinnin' The Webb	Decca/GRP	Chick Webb

Sunny Jain Discography

Artist	Recording	Label	Year

Sunny Jain Collective — *Avaaz* — Sinj Records — 2006
Personnel: Sunny Jain (leader/drumset/dhol/laptop), Rez Abbasi (guitar/sitar guitar), Steve Welsh (tenor & soprano saxophones/effects), Gary Wang (acoustic bass), Samita Sinha (vocals).

Kaash — *Seep* — Sinj Records — 2006
Personnel: Samita Sinha (leader/vocals), Jesse Neuman (trumpet/effects), Dan Fabricatore (electric bass), Sunny Jain (drumset/dhol/laptop).

Steve Blanco Trio — *Contact* — Independent — 2006
Personnel: Steve Blanco (leader/piano), Adam Roberts (acoustic bass), Sunny Jain (drumset).

JC Hopkins Biggish Band — *Underneath A Brooklyn Moon* — Tigerlily Records — 2005
Personnel: JC Hopkins (leader/piano/vocals), Queen Esther (vocals), Lewis "Flip" Barnes (trumpet/vocals), Cleave Guyton (alto saxophone/clarinet), Patience Higgins (tenor saxophone), Claire Daly (baritone saxophone), James Zollar (trumpet), Chuck "Numbers" MacKinnon (trumpet), Vincent Chancey (french horn), J. Walter Hawkes (trombone), Liberty Ellman (guitar), Warren Smith (vibraphone), Catherine Popper (acoustic bass), Sunny Jain (drumset).

Sunny Jain Collective — *Mango Festival* — ZoHo Music — 2004
Personnel: Sunny Jain (leader/drumset), Rez Abbasi (guitar/sitar guitar), Steve Welsh (tenor saxophone/effects). Gary Wang (acoustic bass).

Sunny Jain Collective — *As Is* — NCM East Records — 2002
Personnel: Sunny Jain (leader/drumset), Rez Abbasi (guitar/sitar guitar), Steve Welsh (tenor saxophone/effects). Gary Wang (acoustic bass).

David Cook — *Green* — Independent — 2002
Personnel: David Cook (leader/piano), Adam Roberts (acoustic bass), Bob Reynolds (tenor saxophone), Gavin Creel (vocals), Quincy Davis (drumset), Sunny Jain (drumset).

Sheryl Bailey Quartet — *Reunion of Souls* — Pure Music Records — 2001
Personnel: Sheryl Bailey (leader/guitar), Chris Bergson (guitar), Ashley Turner (acoustic bass), Sunny Jain (drumset).

Chris Bergson — *Wait For Spring* — Juniper Records — 2000
Personnel: Chris Bergson (leader/guitar), Chris Berger (acoustic bass), Neal Miner (acoustic bass), Greg Glassman (trumpet), Joe Strasser (drumset), Sunny Jain (drumset).

Trudi Mann — *…..Mmmmmm….* — Samson Records — 1999
Personnel: Trudi Mann (leader/vocals), Tedd Firth (piano), Saadi Zain (acoustic bass), Sunny Jain (drumset).

Positive Rhythmic Force — *The Question Is* — Boffo Records — 1998
Personnel: Jason Berg (trumpet), Noah Baerman (piano), Ben Tedoff (acoustic bass), Sunny Jain (drumset).

Positive Rhythmic Force — *self-titled* — PRF Records — 1996
Personnel: Jason Berg (trumpet), Noah Baerman (piano), Ben Tedoff (acoustic bass), Sunny Jain (drumset).

Jon Regen Trio — *From Left To Right* — Independent — 1996
Personnel: Jon Regen (leader/piano), Earl May (acoustic bass), Sunny Jain (drumset).

If you love this book, you'll love our schools!

Online...

WorkshopLive

The next generation of music education from the founders of the National Guitar Workshop

Take a FREE online lesson today.
workshoplive.com

...or Near You!

N·G·W
National Guitar Workshop

LOCATIONS: Connecticut, Florida, Seattle, Nashville, Los Angeles, Texas, San Francisco, Virginia

1-800-234-6479
guitarworkshop.com